A Manual
of Sixteenth-Century
Contrapuntal Style

A Manual
of Sixteenth-Century
Contrapuntal Style

Charlotte Smith

DELAWARE
Newark: University of Delaware Press
London and Toronto: Associated University Presses

Associated University Presses
440 Forsgate Drive
Cranbury, NJ 08512

Associated University Presses
25 Sicilian Avenue
London WC1A 2QH, England

Associated University Presses
P.O. Box 488, Port Credit
Mississauga, Ontario
L5G 4M2
Canada L5G 4M2

The paper used in this publication meets the requirements
of the American National Standard for Permanence of Paper
for Printed Library Materials Z39.48-1984.

Library of Congress Cataloging-in-Publication Data

Smith, Charlotte, 1921–
    A manual of sixteenth-century contrapuntal style.

    Bibliography: p.
    Includes index.
    1. Counterpoint.   2. Music—Theory—16th century.
I. Title.
MT55.S63   1989___   781.4'2   87-40064
ISBN 0-87413-327-0 (alk. paper)

Contents

Preface

The singular beauty of Renaissance counterpoint is best understood through an approach that combines the hearing experience with analytical observation of the music as written. The listener of today, in hearing the music of four hundred years ago, may be intrigued by its different qualities, but the source of the difference may be elusive if explanation is sought in terms of more recent music. Yet the resources used by composers of the sixteenth century are not elusive, and one's perceptions in experiencing the music may increase through understanding of the techniques and materials employed by the major composers of the time.

The purpose of this book is to provide guidance in developing understanding of the principles of sixteenth-century contrapuntal composition and to assist in the acquisition of skill in writing within the requirements of the style. The pedagogical approach is derived from a number of firmly held views of the author, the first of which is that the music must be experienced aurally. Singing provides in itself a large measure of understanding of the melodic writing, and sixteenth-century music is significantly appropriate for study through singing. Another view is that the historical approach to studying the style should be considered, but followed only insofar as it produces the desired results. Therefore, the species system, which imposes a disciplined but rigid approach to the study of counterpoint, will not be followed, but its principle of beginning with the simple concepts and moving gradually to the difficult will be maintained. Another view relates to the manner in which the music was notated and its relevance to the notation of today. The historical white mensural notation will be studied, but beginning early and continuing throughout the study, observations will be made on the translation of such notation into the more familiar black-note notation of today. This approach, as the author has experienced it, makes possible through frequent experience in reading and hearing the music in more than one system of notation a natural adjustment to and recognition of the principles of the style regardless of the form of the notation chosen to record them. It provides through experience the knowledge that in sixteenth-century music, rhythm and meter are free of each other, and that there is no aural difference between 2/1, 4/2, and 4/4.

Examples from a variety of composers are included, many of them complete works or movements of works. There is a large degree of commonality among the composers of this period, particularly in their sacred works, and it is in the consistency of style as shown by Palestrina, Lasso, Victoria, and others, that one may identify the compositional procedures that characterize the period. While the strict purity of the vocal works of Palestrina has been the focal point of traditional studies of sixteenth-century music, the works of Lasso in their enormous and relaxed variety merit equal attention. His setting of the *Penitential Psalms* contains in concentrated fashion a plethora of contrapuntal techniques for a variety of voice combinations. Most of its verse settings are short and appropriate for informal reading and analysis. This text will refer to the author's edition of the *Penitential Psalms* for many of its illustrations, and it is recommended that the study be further enriched through use of these miniature contrapuntal masterpieces for analysis and singing of suggested passages.*

Suggestions for writing examples of various aspects of the style are made at appropriate points. An instructor may choose to devise different exercises applicable to the needs perceived close at hand.

The text is aimed toward furthering the musical development of the upper undergraduate or graduate student, but it should also be of interest to anyone with a knowledge of music fundamentals and a desire to delve below the surface beauties of Renaissance polyphony.

The author acknowledges with gratitude the generous assistance of colleagues, students, and friends. Their support, forebearance, unfailing encouragement, and countless valuable suggestions during the months of preparation expedited the completion of the book.

---

*Orlando di Lasso, *Seven Penitential Psalms with Two Laudate Psalms,* ed. Charlotte Smith (Newark, Del.: University of Delaware Press, 1983).

A Manual
of Sixteenth-Century
Contrapuntal Style

1
An Overview of the Style

The Choir

The chapel choir of the sixteenth century consisted exclusively of male voices. The highest-pitched parts were sung by young boys, trained in the cathedral school, with the men singing the lower parts. The parts were designated as *cantus* or *superius* (soprano), *altus, tenor,* and *bassus.* When additional parts were required they were designated as *quintus, sextus, septimus;* they aligned in range with one or more of the other parts as, for example, the second tenor in a modern choir. The choirs seem to have consisted of around twenty to thirty singers and were the best-trained musicians available, many of them composers as well as singers. The function of the choir was to provide music for the daily liturgical services and to assist in festive celebrations.

While an instrumental accompaniment was rarely provided for the singers and parts were generally undesignated for specific instruments, accounts and paintings of the time indicate the use of instruments, probably doubling voice parts. Frequently the singers themselves played instruments and were engaged for a dual role. Therefore the music, while essentially *a cappella,* might have had parts strengthened or colored by the addition of instrumental sound.*

In figure 1 may be seen the Munich chapel choir of Duke Albert V under Orlando di Lasso. The painting by Hans Mielich occupies a full page of the second folio of the manuscript of the *Penitential Psalms.* There are pictured thirty-nine participants of which fifteen have instruments, three are young boy sopranos, and eighteen are adult singers. The remaining three appear to be court dignitaries, the one with rich clothing and medals probably the Duke himself. Although opinions differ on the position of Lasso in the painting, it is more likely because of his honored status at court that he is standing beside the Duke rather than seated at the keyboard.†

---

*See Howard Mayer Brown, "Performing Practice: 15th- and 16th-Century Music," *The New Grove Dictionary of Music and Musicians* (London: Macmillan, 1980), 14:377–83.

†See Walter Frei, "Die Bayerische Hofkapelle unter Orlando di Lasso," *Die Musikforschung* 15 (1962): 352–64.

Figure 1. Orlando di Lasso with the musicians of the Bavarian Court. *(Bayerische Staatsbibliothek, Munich, Mus. MS A, II.)*

Notation and Text Underlay

The notation of sixteenth-century polyphonic ensemble music generally did not include the use of bar-lines and ties, simple devices that aid the present-day musician. Each part was notated on a five-line staff; a variety of clefs was employed, largely to avoid the use of leger lines. The absence of score-arrangement, which would place the voices of a composition in vertical alignment for producing simultaneous notes, is a conspicuous difference between the Renaissance notation and the modern performance edition. Voice parts were written either in separate part-books or in choir-books. In the former, the individual part, tenor for example, for several compositions would be collected in one book. In the choir-books the parts were written on two facing pages, two or more parts on a page. Iconography of the period shows singers gathered around the one book. The margins were frequently adorned with miniature paintings, making the book a treasured possession of its chapel. The two folios of Lasso's setting of the *Penitential Psalms* are extraordinarily beautiful examples of such books. Two pages from the second folio are reproduced in figure 2. Although two or more parts were written on the same page, the singer had only his own part to follow, without the aid of vertical alignment with another part.

The mensural system from the middle of the fifteenth century to the late sixteenth century largely employed note values longer than those generally used in modern notation. The term *white notation* is frequently applied to it, distinguishing it from the black forms of the fourteenth century and of present-day notation. Relations between

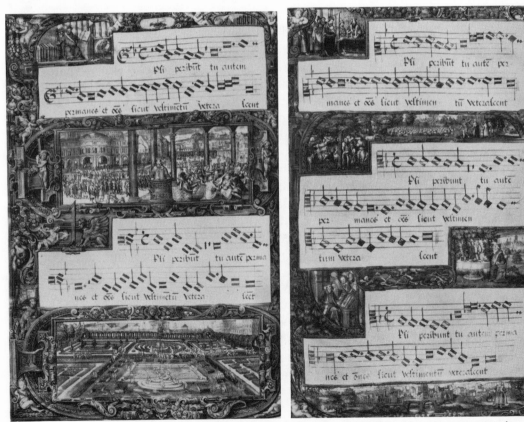

Figure 2. Lasso: *Penitential Psalms*, 5, verse 27, showing the five parts laid out on one opening of the choirbook (*Bayerische Staatsbibliothek, Munich, Mus. MS A, II.*)

note values were regulated by meter signatures and the proportional system, both to be discussed in chapters 2 and 9.

The underlaying of the Latin text in the original manuscripts was frequently incomplete, with extension of themes and motivic recurrence often showing no accompanying words. The division of words into syllables and the placement of syllables in direct relation to the associated notes were left more often to performers, as well as the repeating of phrases of text in melodic extensions. Editors of modern editions have supplied the text in precise relation to the notes.

Performance Practice

To the performer of today, accustomed to modern notation, it might appear that the performer of the sixteenth century, reading his score without the aid of bar-lines, ties, complete accidentals, text underlay, tempo, dynamic and phrasing indications, was presenting music under extraordinarily difficult circumstances. Although the demands on him were large, he was a product of his time, with an understanding gained by listening and participating as much as by instruction in the music of his day. Performers of today frequently speculate about pitch levels in the sixteenth century, but since there was no standard concert pitch as in modern times, there is no certain knowledge to justify a conclusion that a note was higher or lower than its present-day counterpart. A polyphonic composition with a first tenor of high range and a second bass of low range offers little reason to assume that it could have been much higher or much lower than the pitch level of today. Undoubtedly the pitch varied from time to time and from place to place.

The Modal System

The sacred music of the Renaissance was rooted in the ecclesiastical modes, a system of scales found in plainsong or Gregorian chant. The names for the modes were borrowed from the Greek modes by medieval theorists, although the reason for doing so is unclear in that the modes are not the same. Originally only four modes were actually used, each of which was later divided into two forms, a higher called *authentic* and a lower called *plagal*. By the time of Pope Gregory the Great, who reigned from 590 to 604, the system of eight modes was established.

Although the plagal form of a mode had a different range from the corresponding authentic mode (the initial tone of the plagal made was a fourth below that of the authentic), both modes had the same final note (*finalis*), namely the first note of the authentic mode. The plagal forms are indicated by the prefix Hypo- added to the names of the authentic modes, and the modes are numbered in the Roman tradition. One tone of each mode was favored as a chanting or reciting tone, similar in importance to the modern dominant and generally referred to by that name. In the authentic modes it was usually the fifth tone of the mode, while in the plagal modes it was usually a third lower. The variable status of the note B caused modifications in the selection of the dominant, for if heard in relation to F, a tritone resulted. The augmented interval, the so-called *diabolus in musica*, was considered sinister and a sound to be avoided. Therefore the interval was corrected by flattening the B in relation to the F. The modes affected by the use of B-flat were the Phrygian (dominant on C), the Hypophrygian (dominant on A), and the Hypomixolydian (dominant on C). The eight modes used in chant with their finals and dominants are summarized in example 1-1.

Example 1-1

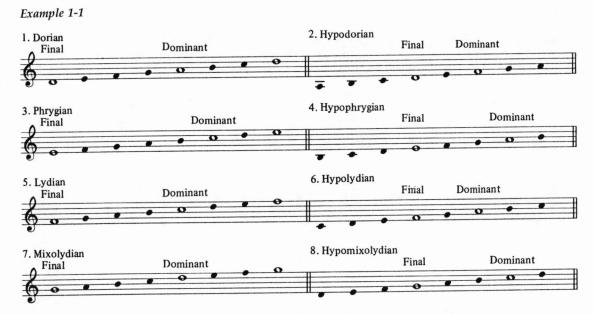

In the following plainsong melodies may be seen the natural rhythm and curve of phrase, stepwise pitch movement, conservative range, and the close relation between text and melodic movement typical of Gregorian chant. Upon singing them one may sense the subtle expression of feeling and the refined character of the art they represent.

Example 1-2

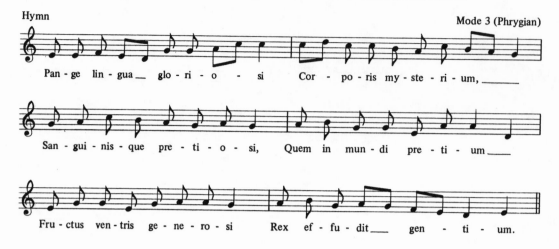

Hymn   Mode 3 (Phrygian)

Pan - ge lin - gua__ glo - ri - o - si   Cor - po - ris my - ste - ri - um,_____

San - gui - nis - que pre - ti - o - si,   Quem in mun - di pre - ti - um____

Fru - ctus ven - tris ge - ne - ro - si   Rex ef - fu - dit__ gen - ti - um.

Antiphon   Mode 5 (Lydian)

Mon - tes et__ om - nes col - les *hu - mi - li - a - bun - tur:

et e - runt pra - va__ in di - rec - ta,_____ et__ a - spe - ra in vi - as__ pla - nas:

ve - ni Do - mi - ne,_____ et no - li tar - da - re, al - le - lu - ia.

Hymn   Mode 8 (Hypomixolydian)

Ve - ni Cre - a - tor__ Spi - ri - tus, Men - tes tu - o - rum__ vi - si - ta:

Im - ple__ su - per - na gra - ti - a   Quae__ tu cre - a - sti_____ pec - to - ra.

The use of B♭ gradually brought about an awareness of two other modes, the Aeolian and the Ionian. The Dorian mode with consistent B♭s became the Aeolian mode, and the Lydian with consistent B♭s became the Ionian mode. The two, Aeolian and Ionian, with their corresponding plagal modes, were not officially recognized until the sixteenth century. The Aeolian and Hypoaeolian were numbered 9 and 10. Modes 11 and 12, the Locrian and Hypolocrian, were not used because of tritone and cadential problems. The Ionian and Hypoionian modes were numbered 13 and 14.

The Ionian is the same as the major scale that was to be favored by composers in later centuries, and the Aeolian became the pure minor scale. Although ignored in chant and not favored by Renaissance composers, these two modes ultimately provided the basis for the later major-minor system of tonality which undergirds most of the music since the 1700s.

The rich body of Gregorian chant was used by composers of the sixteenth century as a resource for melody on which to build larger compositions. The writing of counterpoint, literally the combining of melodies for two or more voices, brought about changes in the modal system. While the authentic and plagal forms of the modes as used in chant were different scales with different dominants, the act of combining melodies for voices of different range created the necessity of having all voices in a composition observe the same dominant, that of the authentic mode. With voice parts normally a fourth apart, the use of the plagal mode became in polyphony merely a matter of range. The chant melody, or *cantus firmus,* was usually placed in the tenor; the beginning of the composition frequently stated the mode by introducing the final or dominant as the initial note, with other voices imitating at the fourth or fifth; the last bass note was generally the final of the mode.

In some compositions the beginning pitch does not express the mode, and often the cause is the use of a plainsong theme which itself did not begin with the final or the dominant. For example, in plainsong the initial note in a Hypophrygian melody is frequently F. Composers using such melodies may imitate the F with C, thus obscuring the identity of the mode even more. The final cadence is a more reliable indicator of the mode, although exceptions are found there, too. In compositions in the Lydian mode the final cadence is sometimes on A instead of F, possibly because of tritone problems in cadencing on F.

Transposition

The entire modal system could be transposed up a fourth or down a fifth from its normal range by the inclusion of B♭ in the signature. Thus, the Dorian mode would start on G, the others following in order. The tritone in the transposed modes appears between B♭ and E, and is corrected by the flattening of E. While the signature of B♭ is evidence of transposition, it would be natural for singers of any era to change the pitch level of a written piece simply by singing it higher or lower without written transposition.

Accidentals *(Musica Ficta)*

Although B♭ was the only accidental used in chant, with the advent of polyphony other accidentals were added. The use of these accidentals was called *musica ficta* (false music), because for a long time such accidentals did not appear in written music but were added by performers according to certain practices that were understood by them.* Respect for the purity of the modes was required by ecclesiastical tradition, and long after the restrictions disappeared the custom of letting the performers add chromatic changes remained. Composers sometimes wrote the accidentals in the music, and editors of modern editions have added others according to their judgment and knowledge of the style.† Editorial accidentals are written above the affected notes.

---

*Brown, "Performing Practice," pp. 377–83.

†A further commentary on *musica ficta* may be found in Nicholas Routley, "A Practical Guide to *Musica Ficta,*" *Early Music* 13, no. 1 (1985): 59–71; and John Caldwell, "*Musica Ficta,*" *Early Music* 13, no. 3 (1985): 407–8.

The accidentals used in addition to B♭ were C♯, F♯, and G♯ in both the untransposed and the transposed modes. In the latter, E♭ was used to correct the tritone. The reasons for adding the inflections were varied, and since at first they were frowned on by church authorities, the evidence of their use is uneven. It is certain that the tritone from F to B was corrected by the use of B♭, rarely by F♯; in the transposed modes the tritone from B♭ to E was corrected by the use of E♭. The raised notes were employed mainly in forming the cadences. The natural half-step movement into the final note in the Lydian and Ionian modes was imitated in the other modes by moving F♯ to G, G♯ to A, and C♯ to D. When a melody ascended stepwise to a cadence on A, both F and G were raised to avoid an augmented second from F to G♯. The major third was preferred in final chords, and in the Dorian, Phrygian, and Aeolian modes the minor third was raised by the addition of F♯, G♯, and C♯. These accidentals were also used to affect half-step movement in an imitating voice where the preceding voice contained a natural half step.

Although other accidentals may be found in sixteenth-century music, only B♭, F♯, C♯, and G♯ were regularly used in untransposed modes, with the addition of E♭ in transposed modes. No augmented or diminished intervals were allowed, as the correcting of the tritone would indicate.

In example 1-3A, the tritone is corrected; in Example 1-3B, a leading tone to A is created, requiring consecutive accidentals to avoid an augmented second; in example 1-3C, the third of a final chord is made major.

Example 1-3

Cadence and Modulation

Melodically, the term cadence (from *cadere*, to fall) applies to the bringing of a phrase to its conclusion. In plainsong the voice descended, or "fell," one degree to its final. When a second voice was added, it was found that an approach to the final from below was satisfactory, particularly with the addition of musica ficta to make the approach by half step. The approach to the Ionian and Lydian finals was naturally possible with the second modal degree already a whole step above the final and the seventh a half step below. The Dorian, Mixolydian, and Aeolian, with the addition of an accidental to the seventh modal degree, achieved a similar approach to the final. The Phrygian remained different from the others, lacking a D♯ to create a half step from below and having already a half step above the final. In the Phrygian cadence on E with two or more voices, the descending half step F–E is usually in the lowest voice and the ascending whole step D–E is in an upper voice. Phrygian melody has a distinct quality of inconclusiveness because of its lack of an ascending half step to the final. The use of F♯ is inappropriate in the Phrygian cadence, and as there is no major dominant triad on B to lead to E, the cadence cannot have the authentic sound of the other modes. B, as the fifth modal degree, however, has prominence as a melodic tone.

The cadence on D, for example, is not confined to the Dorian mode in which it is the final but appears in other modes, and there is likewise a sense of commonality among cadences in most of the modes. Consequently the sense of final or, to the modern ear, "key," is made vague by the willingness of the modal system to accommodate a variety of cadence points within one composition. "Modulation," meaning change of key, is rarely felt in polyphony, although it existed in plainsong. However, cadences on notes other than the final, or even the dominant, are frequently heard in polyphony, but the original mode usually is resumed after the cadence. Some cadence points were favored by specific modes more than others, and a list of cadence points used by each mode is included in chapter 5.

Practical Considerations

It is in recognizing that hearing music is essential to understanding music, that it is recommended that the study of Renaissance counterpoint be based on frequent aural experience with the style. Singing, with available instruments at times reinforcing vocal parts or substituting for missing singers, can bring an understanding and excitement to the study that talking about it cannot alone achieve. Starting with duos, the singing-hearing experience should progress to five- and six-voice polyphony, with instruments assisting when desired or needed to complete the parts. A variety of compositions for singing are included in this manual, with references made to others that are easily available, particularly to the motets of the *Penitential Psalms* of Lasso, which are practical in their brevity and generally undemanding tessitura.

To facilitate the reading of the music, this manual will employ only the familiar treble and bass clefs, with the tenor voices designated by the treble clef with subscript 8, indicating that the actual sound is an octave lower. The historic "white-note" notation will be used in the beginning examples, but examples will be gradually introduced in familiar "black-note" notation to help the reader to understand and become adept at interpreting the old notation in modern symbols. Many complete compositions for singing will be in practical modern notation, as is also the edition of the Lasso *Penitential Psalms* to which reference is frequently made. Bar lines will be used throughout the manual. There is no totally satisfactory substitute for them, even though the "Mensurstrich," a line drawn partly through the staff or between staves, is preferred in some editions. The Mensurstrich has the disadvantages of being more difficult to read, of disrupting the text, and of making problems when different mensurations occur in various voices. The study of melody and rhythm should make clear that the bar line is used for facilitating reading and should not affect metrical design or stress.

Today one may easily transpose the modes by observing the similarity of the system to the C major scale. The Dorian series of pitches can be found by starting on scale step 2 of C major, the Phrygian by starting on 3, and the others in order through the Ionian on C. This would hold true in relation to any major scale, because other than in highness or lowness of range there is no aural difference between a transposed mode and an untransposed mode.

It can be helpful in developing aural recognition of the individual modes to compare them with the familiar major and minor scales. The Ionian is the major scale; the Aeolian is the pure minor scale; Dorian has the sound of pure minor with raised sixth degree; Phrygian has the sound of pure minor with lowered second degree; Lydian is like the major with raised fourth degree, and Mixolydian is like the major with lowered seventh degree.

EXERCISE

1. Sing the modes; learn their dominants.

2. Sing the Gregorian melodies in Example 1-2 until they are familiar, noting their

dominants, leaps, ranges, B♭, melisma, rhythmic freedom.

3. Sing transposed modes.

4. Each of the Psalms in the *Penitential Psalms* of Lasso is in a different mode. Examine the initial notes of the various sections. Do they suggest the mode? Are they always the final or the dominant?

Latin Pronunciation

Classical Latin and ecclesiastical Latin differ slightly in their pronunciation, in that the latter through centuries of use in the Roman liturgy has been somewhat affected by the Italian language.

The Latin vowels are each enunciated as one single pure sound. In English, vowels are often mixed or uttered in sequence, modified by their position in regard to adjacent consonants. The Latin vowel, however, must have no alteration in its timbre during its articulation, whether it is long or short. The following suggestions are offered as a guide in singing Latin texts.

Single Vowels

A   as in *father*
E   as in *red*
I   as in the *ee* sound in *feet*
O   as in *for*
U   as in *moon*
Y   as the Latin *i*

Consecutive Vowels

As a rule two or three consecutive vowels retain their own sounds, which are pronounced separately.

E. g., Filii, fi-li-i
   Ait, a-it
   Prout, pro-ut

Exceptions:

AE and OE: pronounced as the Latin *e*.
AU, EU, AY: the two vowels form one syllable but both vowels must be heard. The emphasis is on the first vowel.
U followed by another vowel and preceded by NG or Q: the emphasis is on the second vowel and is uttered as one syllable.

Consonants

C before e, ae, oe, i, y: ch as in *church*
CC before e, ae, oe, i, y: t-ch
SC before e, ae, oe, i, y: sh as in *shed*

C in all other cases: as the English *k*
CH as the English *k*
G before e, ae, oe, i, y: soft G as in *generous*
G in all other cases: hard G as in *government*
GN ny as in *canyon*
H mute except in *mihi* (mee-kee) and *nihil* (nee-keel)
J treated as Y, forming one sound with the following vowel
R slightly rolled
S as in *sit*
TI before a vowel and preceded by any letter except S, T, or X: SEE
TH as the English *t*
X *ks* (as in English).
XC before e, ae, oe, i, y: *ksh*
Z *dz*
All other consonants: as in English
Double consonants must be clearly sounded.

2
Rhythm

Contrapuntal Accentuation

A subtle system of accentuation existed during the sixteenth century that created a sense of stress on a longer note in the vicinity of shorter notes. The note, either preceded or followed by notes of smaller value than itself, seemed to have force in that it temporarily interrupted movement although no dynamic increase was involved. The listener sensed strength in the longer note, a sense of quantitative reinforcement. Such implied stress through duration, called agogic accent, could be felt within a single melodic line; it was also significant in creating an effect of cross rhythms between voice parts where the longer notes in one voice part claimed attention from the shorter note values in another voice part.

Although there were no bar lines, there was an organization of beats, a governing scheme for the placement of dissonances, cadences, phrase beginnings and endings. This regulating system, or primary rhythm, was represented by the meter symbol but not dictated by it. The quantitative stress (agogic accent), or secondary rhythm, was irregular, reflecting the prose rhythm with its varied syllabic stresses.* Composers were adept at contrasting a rhythmical accent created by dissonance on specific beats with an irregular agogic accent between parts. This sense of rhythmical conflict, offsetting the predictable with the unpredictable, is one of the most intriguing and vital aspects of sixteenth-century music.

Example 2-1 illustrates the interaction of the voice parts, each having its own variety of stress design but moving nevertheless within a larger design. Long notes are present

Example 2-1
Lasso: *Christe redemptor omnium* (hymn)

---

*A detailed discussion of the perception of accent may be found in Knud Jeppesen, *The Style of Palestrina and the Dissonance*, trans. Margaret Hamerik (1946; reprint, New York: Dover Publications, 1970), pp. 18–30.

which promote the suggestion of stress by duration, in contrast to the shorter notes surrounding them. Long notes sometimes begin on a normally weak part of the measure causing a momentary conflict between the primary and the secondary rhythm.

Generally, the words of the text suggest the rhythmical design of the music. However, when there is a conflict between the prose rhythm and the musical requirements, the musical requirements are likely to take precedence.

Note Values and Rests

From the mid-fifteenth century to the late sixteenth century a system of note values with open-headed symbols was used, which has come to be called white mensural notation. This designation refers to the frequency of the use of the half note and longer values and also to the change from the black form of the preceding period. The following durations were used:

Example 2-2

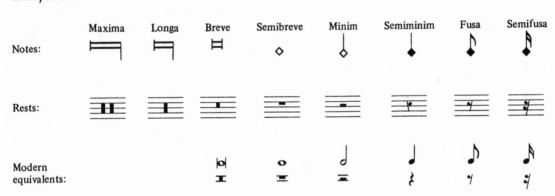

In addition to the single symbols of notation, certain symbols called ligatures were used that combined two or more tones and indicated they were to be slurred and executed in one breath on one syllable of text. Their presence in a manuscript source is indicated in a modern edition by the placement of brackets above the staff. They were used abundantly from the earliest stages of polyphonic music into the fifteenth century but gradually disappeared toward the end of the sixteenth century.

The maxima was seldom used, appearing in such instances as a final note or representing a voice part augmenting the note values of another part. The longa also was useful for notating the final tone of a voice part that was to be sustained. The semifusa was rarely used in ecclesiastical music. Ligatures were a part of the sixteenth-century manuscript and are mentioned here because they belong to the study of the style. They are not, however, for practical usage today.

Meter Signatures

The meter signature most often used was ¢, which would be equivalent to present-day 2/1 meter. While the major pulse of the measure is felt on the two semibreves, or two whole notes, the subdivision of the whole notes into half notes, creating a 4/2 meter, is a more practical plan for the assignment of dissonance and consonance. It is 4/2 and its equivalent in modern notation, 4/4, that we shall use for the larger part of this study, with the metric signature ₵ representing four half notes in 4/2 time (and four quarter notes in 4/4 time). From this point on in the study we shall refer to note values smaller than the breve as whole notes, half notes, quarter notes, and eighth notes.

Tempo

Throughout the sixteenth century there was a general uniform sense of tempo or beat in music, referred to as the *tactus*. It was represented by the whole note (semibreve) in duple time.* The duration of a note could be changed by altering the proportional relationships of notes to the beat. The proportional signs used to achieve such changes represent note value changes of mathematical exactness. The composer was not dependent upon a conductor's mood or sense of quickening or lessening of speed as a means of interpreting the music. The relationship of note values to the beat could be changed when the composer wished by introducing triple meter within a composition in duple meter. The use of white mensural notation did not imply a slow beat; probably to the sixteenth-century composer a whole note meant very much what a half note means today and, with proportional change, could approximate a quarter note. The usual present-day tendency to interpret the half note and the whole note as "slow" is one of the reasons that recently published editions of sixteenth-century music frequently present ₵ as 4/4 rather than 4/2. Theoretical treatises of the sixteenth century often contain explanations of the tactus as, for example, the pulse of a man breathing normally, but to convey in words an exact description of tempo was not a possibility. It is thought that the tactus was a slow to moderate beat, making the whole note about M.M. 60–70. That the general sense of beat was unvarying is unlikely, but that there was a common view of the nature of the beat is indicated by the writings of the time.†

Dots and Ties

The basic means of altering the duration of a note in a sixteenth-century manuscript was through the addition of a dot which caused the length of the note to be increased by one-half its value. Without bar lines there was no reason for using the tie, but with the present-day use of bar lines the tie is the means of increasing the note length beyond the measure limitation. The following observations deal with the specific procedures for rhythmic notation in ₵ (4/2) meter:

1. The composition must begin with values no shorter than a dotted half note.
2. The final note of a composition must be no shorter than a breve.
3. Note values of equal length may be tied to each other.
4. Note values may be tied to half their value, the larger note first, except at the end of a phrase or at a final cadence when a whole note may be tied to a breve.
5. Dotted whole notes occur only on beats one and three. To place a dotted whole note on beat two would be comparable to tying a half note from beat four across the bar line to a whole note on beat one, disturbing the sense of primary rhythm.
6. The half note may be tied to a quarter note, but a quarter note is rarely tied to another quarter note. The effect tends to create a type of syncopation that is usually not appropriate to the sacred text.

---

*A further discussion of the tactus may be found in Howard Mayer Brown, "Tactus," *The New Grove Dictionary of Music and Musicians* (London: Macmillan, 1980), 18:518.

†See Willi Apel, *The Notation of Polyphonic Music, 900–1600*, 5th ed. (Cambridge, Mass.: Medieval Academy of America, 1961), pp. 188–191.

7. Eighth notes are not tied.

8. Dotted notes are not tied. (In triple time they may be tied).

9. Rests are initiated on beats one and three, not on two or four. The quarter-note rest is rarely used in the vocal sacred music.

Each of the above observations may be realized in 4/4 time by halving the note values named.

In the following example from Palestrina are many of the features of the style presented thus far. In example 2-3A the meter signature is interpreted in relation to the breve. In example 2-3B the meter is interpreted in relation to the whole note. Upon singing the two versions it will be apparent that there is no aural difference between the two interpretations, that the halving of the note values affects only the visual aspect. The following features should be observed:

1. Primary rhythm
2. Agogic accent
3. Tying
4. Cross rhythm between parts
5. Musica ficta

Example 2-3A

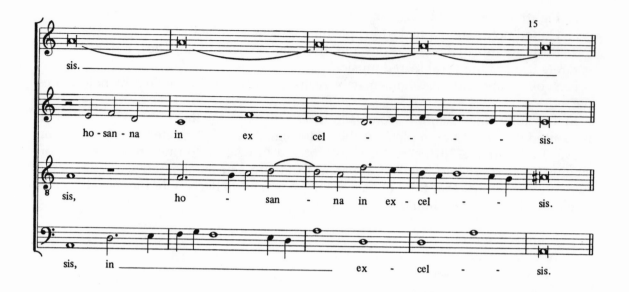

Example 2-3B

Palestrina: Hosanna *(Missa de feria)*

sis. _____

ho - san - na in ex - cel - - - sis.

sis, ho - san - na in ex - cel - - sis.

sis, in _____ ex - cel - - sis.

EXERCISES

1. Learn the rules for tying.

2. From the *Penitential Psalms* of Lasso, sing Psalm VII, verse 7 (p. 246). Notice that the text speaks of the psalmist's urgency for a speedy response from his God. Find instances of unusual relationships of note values. The text might give reason for these exceptions to normal rhythmic arrangements. Sing the brief motet several times until the music seems to move easily with the words and rhythm. Notice the sense of syncopation resulting from tying into half beats as it differs from the gentle cross rhythms and agogic accents of the Palestrina Hosanna.

3. Observe the rhythm of the following "melody," identifying errors in rhythm and notation.

Example 2-4

3
Melody

Vocal Qualities

Melody in sixteenth-century music is essentially vocal melody, reflecting the range and natural tendencies of the human voice. Stepwise movement is far more frequent than leaps; small leaps are more frequent than large; and a regard for tessitura is generally apparent. The flowing line, the balance in rise and fall of pitch level, the restrained use of high and low points combine to create a sense of appropriate enhancement of the religious message of the text.

The fact that melody and rhythm are inseparable creates a difficulty in identifying the qualities of the one without the other. That a note approached by ascending leap conveys the impression of an accent is the reason for some of the restrictions on ascending leaps. The melodic material frequently has its origin in Gregorian chant, and melodies not borrowed from chant include familiar features of chant in the expression of the modes, prose rhythm, and predominance of stepwise movement. The voices are given about the same amount of responsibility in a polyphonic composition, with no one voice generally dominating. Observe in the following melodies from Victoria the preponderance of stepwise movement, the overall melodic contour, and the appropriateness of the rhythm to the text.

Example 3-1
Victoria: *Nisi Dominus* (psalm)

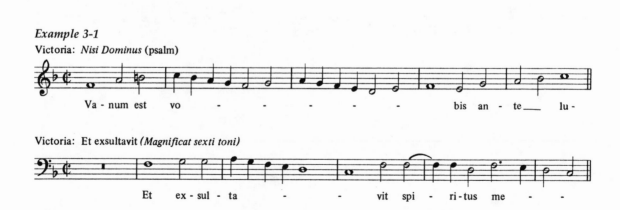

Victoria: Et exsultavit *(Magnificat sexti toni)*

28

Intervals

Although the music is predominantly stepwise, specific leaps are used. The following are observations as to their frequency of use.

1. Major and minor seconds, ascending and descending, are frequently used.
2. Major and minor thirds, ascending and descending, are frequently used.
3. Perfect fourths and fifths, ascending and descending, are frequently used.
4. Minor sixths, ascending only, are infrequently used.
5. Major sixths, ascending only, are rarely used.
6. Perfect octaves, ascending and descending, are infrequently used.
7. Sevenths are not used.
8. Augmented, diminished, and chromatic intervals are not used. They may be found, however, between the ending of one section and the beginning of another. The F to B tritone is corrected by the use of B♭, rarely by F♯, and the tritone in the transposed modes, B♭ to E, is corrected by flattening the E. When the two notes of the tritone are not consecutive, but are heard as the high and low points of a phrase, the correcting accidental is applied, as shown in example 3-2A. When there is cause for a stress to be felt on the two pitches of the tritone, the correcting flat is applied, even though the notes are not adjacent, as shown in example 3-2B.

Example 3-2

Extended Range

Because of the predominantly stepwise motion, extended passages that are initiated near the lower or upper limits of a vocal range may progress in the same direction through the scope of the range if the musical interest or the extension of a syllable of text justifies it. The long passages without directional change, however, are far less frequent than passages of fewer notes, as seen in example 3-3.

Example 3-3
Lasso: Gloria *(Missa Puis que i'ay perdu)*

Fi - li - us   Pa -   -   -   -   -   -   tris.

Treatment of Leaps

The consideration of leaps involving the breve, the whole note, and the half note will be made at this point. The study of the subdivisions of the half note will be included in chapter 6.

An ascending stepwise melodic line does not generally precede an ascending leap, and likewise a descending stepwise line is not likely to precede a descending leap. A single leap is generally preceded and followed by movement in the opposite direction of the leap. Exceptions may be found, particularly when the leap is not larger than a third.

The larger the leap, the more likely it will be followed by a change in direction that, in a sense, tends to fill in the leap.

Example 3-4
Palestrina: Sanctus *(Missa L'homme armé)*

Successive leaps in the same direction may occur, generally preceded and followed by stepwise motion in the opposite direction of the leaps. They usually follow triadic lines as summarized below:

1. An ascending or descending perfect fifth followed by a perfect fourth (example 3-5A).

2. An ascending or descending perfect fourth followed by a perfect fifth (example 3-5B). These two pairs of leaps are found most often in the bass.

3. The outline of the three notes of a major or minor triad, including the first and second inversions (example 3-5C).

4. The ascending leap of a perfect fifth followed by a minor third, rarely a major third, found in the Dorian mode (example 3-5D). Rarely found is the descending perfect fifth followed by a third.

5. Two perfect fourths or two perfect fifths in the same direction are sometimes encountered, usually in the bass in long time-values (example 3-5E).

Example 3-5
Palestrina: Sanctus *(Missa brevis)*   Victoria: *Salve Regina* (antiphon)

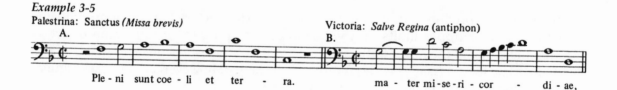

Victoria: *In festo Confessorum Pontificum* (motet)   Lasso: *Penitential Psalms*, VIII, verse 1

Ibid., verse 4   Ibid., II, verse 14

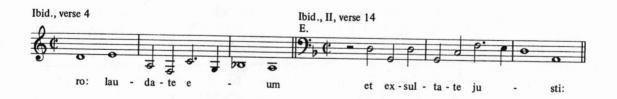

Repeated Notes

The use of repeated notes is generally prompted by the nature of the text. A text of declamatory character, such as the *Improperia*, is likely to have many repeated notes. Within the longer movements of the Mass, homorhythmic sections frequently occur in which there are repeated notes, but their number is small. Repeated notes, though useful at times, are not characteristic of polyphonic texture. Varying their length gives rhythmic diversity, but except with reciting or declamatory texts, the linear flow of melody is better sustained by notes of long duration that are not subdivided into small repetitions. The following passage from Palestrina is an example of homorhythmic movement with a few repeated notes. The Masses contain many such passages.

Example 3-6
Palestrina: Credo *(Missa Sacerdotes Domini)*

In the Lasso *Penitential Psalms,* I, verse 2 begins with the words "Miserere mei Domine," set in a repeated chanting manner in the lower range of the soprano and imitated in the lower range of each of the five voices. The repetition reinforces the suggestion of prayerful penitence.

The following four-voice passage from a motet by Victoria should be sung, attention being given to the skill with which the repeated pitches in one part are frequently present in a texture where other parts are sustaining longer note values, giving balance to the primary and secondary rhythm.

Example 3-7
Victoria: *Sancta Maria, succurre miseris* (motet)

Style and Contour

There is a balance and subtlety in the individual vocal lines that account in large part for the richness of texture created as the voices interact in polyphony. Written to be performed without the aid of instrumental accompaniment, each part has an important contribution to make. In listening to sixteenth-century music one has the awareness of alternating melodic rise and fall among the voices, and an examination of an individual melodic line reveals the same sense of rise and fall: gentle, without the dramatic intensity of the full-choir fortissimo passages of later choral music. Extremes of range are used prudently, and other resources are carefully expended as the text makes appropriate. Phrases are generally long, particularly in sections where one syllable of text is extended over many notes. The preponderance of stepwise movement enhances the sense of flow with an economy of means.

The observations made about the style up to this point can best be understood by analyzing and hearing the music. In addition to the examples provided in these pages, it is suggested that the following motets from the *Penitential Psalms* be studied and sung, remembering that the comments made on note values in relation to the breve are here interpreted in relation to the whole note. While familiarity with the style is developing through singing the music, further enrichment may be gained by listening to a variety of vocal combinations, ranges, and types of text. The modes, musica ficta, and melodic and rhythmic movement can all be experienced in these short motets. The modal scheme of the psalm settings—Psalm I in Mode 1, Psalm II in Mode 2, and on through Psalm VIII in Mode 8—affords an excellent opportunity to observe the features of each mode, their differences and similarities.

Psalm I, verse 3 (p. 21).
Psalm I, verse 9 (p. 34).
Psalm III, verse 8 (p. 96).
Psalm III, verse 24 (p. 127).
Psalm IV, no. 9 (p. 144).

4
Beginning Melody Writing

Preliminary Observations

The writing of counterpoint has been greatly influenced by the famous *Gradus ad Parnassum* by Johann Joseph Fux. Published in Vienna in 1725, the counterpoint manual became a primary influence in the training of composers in contrapuntal composition for over a century, and remains useful even now. Its usefulness has been attested to by many composers, including Haydn and Mozart.

Fux introduced for the writing of counterpoint a plan for developing disciplined skill while progressing from the simple to the complex. His approach was particularly suitable to instruction in counterpoint, the term itself derived from *punctus contra punctum*, i.e., "note against note," or correspondingly, melody against melody. Claiming his sense of style was derived from his study of Palestrina, he began his instruction with two-part counterpoint, continuing on to three- and four-part writing, and then on to further complexities. For each level he introduced a series of five exercises, or *species*, which provided a systematic approach to mastering the difficulties in one level before moving to the next. In the first species, a melody was written in whole notes and treated as a cantus firmus, or borrowed melody, above which another voice was to be added in consonant relationship, "note against note." He continued methodically, adding in the second species two half notes to each whole note in the cantus firmus. Dissonance was introduced on the unaccented beats. In the third species, four quarter notes were written against each whole note of the cantus firmus. In the fourth species, half notes were again introduced, tied from unaccented beats to accented beats, at times creating suspensions against the whole notes of the cantus firmus. In the fifth species, additional rhythmic arrangements were introduced against the whole note.

Although generations of composers and teachers have praised Fux, major objections have been raised against him in recent times. Critics suspect that his rigidity inhibits rhythmic and melodic flexibility and that the methodical restraints produce unmusical results. There is something to be said, however, for an approach that assures graded progress from the easy to the difficult and that allows the melodic elements to be grasped before rhythmic complexities are encountered.

While the species system will not be followed in this manual, the beginning writing of both melody and counterpoint will follow the traditional pedagogical precedent of using only breves, whole notes, and half notes. The rhythm will not be frozen, however, into a succession of whole notes, nor will the writing be limited to white notes for any longer than is necessary to gain a perception of the basic requirements of the style.

Vocal Range

Each voice part was composed within the limitations of vocal range and with the recognition of the limitation of tessitura, that area within the range where more of the pitches are placed. While extremes of range are employed in sixteenth-century melody, the voice is not required to remain within the extreme areas, and the beauty and serenity of the sound is enhanced by such vocal considerations. Vocal ranges and tessituras generally employed are shown in example 4-1.

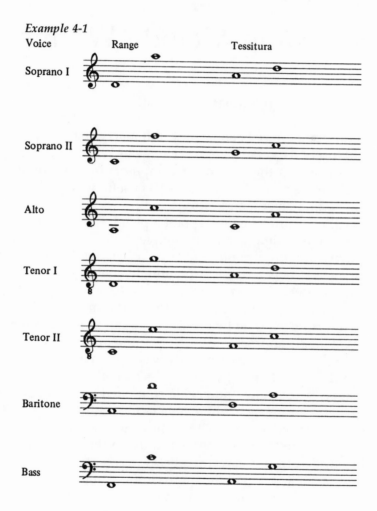

Example 4-1

Initial Tones and Cadences

The mode in which a melody is written is often expressed in the beginning pitches. Starting on the first beat with a whole note or longer value the initial pitch is likely to be the first or fifth degree of the mode—except for the Phrygian mode, where the beginning tone may be the first, fourth, or fifth degree. In polyphony the ranges of neighboring voices often cause melodies to express the compass of both authentic and plagal forms simultaneously. The compass of the tenor part is traditionally the determining factor in designating the mode of a polyphonic piece. This practice derives from earlier times when the tenor was assigned the plainsong melody. The last note of the bass part is generally the final of the mode.

The phrase endings, or cadences, also occur at points that traditionally are appropriate to the particular mode of the composition. Final cadences are generally on the final of the mode, while interior cadences may be on the final, the dominant, or other points of the mode. Phrygian and Aeolian melodies prefer the fourth degree instead of the fifth, with the third degree next in order of preference. The following chart lists beginning notes and cadence points for each of the modes.*

MODE	INITIAL NOTES	COMMON CADENCES	LESS COMMON CADENCES	RARE CADENCES
Dorian	D,A	D,A,F	G,C	E
Phrygian	E,A,B,	E,A,G,	D,C	F
Lydian	F,C	F,C	A,D	
Mixo-lydian	G,D	G,D,C	A	F,E
Aeolian	A,E	A,D,C	G,F	E
Ionian	C,G	C,G,A	D	F,E

The variety of cadence points adds a richness to the modal sound in somewhat the same sense that modulation varies the key of a modern composition. A cadence is made convincing by the use of a leading tone, and when the ascending half step to the cadence point is not present in the mode, it is created by the use of musica ficta. Therefore, in the Dorian mode, the approach to a cadence on D would contain C♯, and within the same mode might also be heard cadences on A with G♯, on G with F♯, and cadences on F and C approached by their natural leading tones. The added color of the cadence points heightens the interpretation of the text and the sense of phrase ending, while at the same time expanding the tonal resources of the modes.

The cadence points, except for the cadence on E, were approached by descending whole step and by ascending half step. The approach to E reverses the position of the half and whole steps, with E approached from above by half step and from below by whole step. The nature of the Phrygian mode with its half step above the final is never disturbed by sharpening D to lead up to E.

The Lydian mode with its frequent B♭ may appear to be the Ionian. An example of this suggestion is found in the fifth psalm of Lasso's setting of the *Penitential Psalms*. Psalm V is in Mode 5, the Lydian mode, yet the presence of B♭ in the signature would suggest a

*According to the findings of Knud Jeppesen, *Counterpoint: The Polyphonic Vocal Style of the Sixteenth Century*, trans. Glen Haydon (Englewood Cliffs, N.J.: Prentice-Hall, 1939), pp. 81–82; and Gustave Soderlund, *Direct Approach to Counterpoint in Sixteenth-Century Style* (Englewood Cliffs, N.J.: Prentice-Hall, 1947), pp. 15–17.

transposed mode. It is not transposed, however, but is Lydian on F with B♭ placed in the signature instead of beside B within the voice parts. When approaching a cadence on C, B♭ is raised to become a leading tone.

Three melodies from Victoria are quoted in example 4-2. Example 4-2A is a Phrygian melody beginning on A. Example 4-2B is in the transposed Dorian mode, with musica ficta creating a leading tone to G. In example 4-2C, also in the Dorian mode, E♭ is used to correct the tritone in proximity to B♭. It would be helpful to sing the melodies, observing the phrase beginnings, the cadences, the accidentals, and the overall contour, rhythm, and text setting.

Example 4-2

Victoria: Et misericordia *(Magnificat tertii toni)*

A.

Et mi - se - ri - cor - di - a e - - - - ius.

Victoria: Et exsultavit *(Magnificat primi toni)*

B.

Et ex - sul - ta - - - - - - vit.

Victoria: Credo *(Missa Gaudeamus)*

C.

Et in Spi - ri - tum san - ctum Do - - - mi - num,____

Contour and Rhythmic Aspects

The sixteenth-century style of melody is basically stepwise, creating a sense of long flowing phrases with proselike rhythms. The strict attention to the use of leaps, the absence of chromaticism and of augmented and diminished intervals, the subtlety of the primary and secondary rhythms, and the rarity of sequential repetition contribute to the perception of grace and naturalness in the style. A melody usually starts in long time-values, gradually increases activity as though gaining momentum with shorter note-values, and then tapers off as it approaches a cadence. The pitch successions, in addition to the restrained use of leaps, are balanced in their use of high and low points. The established peaks of the melody are not overstated by repetition; ascending motion is balanced by descending motion; and leaps are compensated for by stepwise movement.

Text Setting

The prose rhythm of the Latin text generally provided the design of accentuation for the sacred vocal music. The impression of accent could be achieved by the subtle means of relative placement of notes. Notes that are higher or longer than the notes immediately around them, or notes whose approach by leap interrupts a stepwise passage, tend to sound accented although no stress has been applied to them. The important syllable of a significant word in the text is likely to be placed at such points. Another means of implied stress was the practice of having the vowel of an important syllable extend through a series of notes, such extension being referred to as a *melisma*. Any white note may carry a syllable of text, and repeated white notes must each carry a syllable. The last syllable of the text must coincide with the final note. The requirements for use of text with subdivisions of the half note are somewhat different and will be discussed in chapter 6. Observe in example 4-3 the suggestion of the prose rhythm in the unity of the syllables and the rhythmic scheme of the pitches. Notice the repetition and extension of short phrases of text.

Example 4-3
Victoria: *In Purificatione Beatas Mariae* (motet)

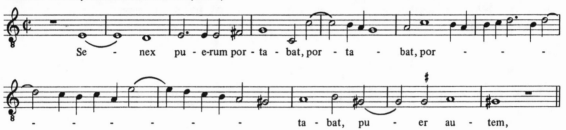

Summary and Application

A review of the discussion of rhythm and melody in chapters 2 and 3 would be beneficial. The writing of a simple melody in white notes should employ the information presented thus far and, with text, achieve an interesting musical result.

In preparation for writing a melody following the above recommended review these guidelines should be observed:

1. Read the text aloud several times to sense the prose rhythm and locate the important words and their stressed syllables.

2. Select a mode whose qualities seem appropriate for the nature of the text.

3. Decide upon the voice part for which the melody is to be written and review its range. Remember the importance of tessitura.

4. Stepwise motion should predominate, but leaps are needed, particularly as a means of implying stress on important syllables and varying the pitch area of a phrase. Remember that a leap is generally approached and left in the opposite direction to that of the leap. Consecutive leaps should follow a triad line, or an octave with intervening fourth or fifth, and should be approached and left in the opposite direction to the leaps.

5. The augmented fourth, F to B, should be corrected by flattening B, and the augmented fourth in the transposed modes, B♭ to E, should be corrected by flattening E.

6. Begin the melody on a pitch appropriate to the mode as suggested in the list of initial notes. In addition to the final, the melody requires the use of the dominant as a focal point within the phrase. Otherwise a sense of melodic direction may be lacking until the approach to the cadence.

7. The significance of the high point and the low point of the phrase may be weakened by repetition. Returning to a peak pitch over and over takes from its signifi-

cance, as may also the repeating of an arpeggiated triad. The text generally suggests the employment of a variety of resources, and the use of the dominant, or reciting tone, as a secondary focal point helps to unify the melody.

8. In general, begin slowly, gain momentum, decrease activity toward the cadence.

9. Approach the cadence by step from above or by half step from below, raising F, C, and G as needed. The Phrygian cadence point has its half step above the final, and no accidentals are used. A cadence on A may be approached from B or G♯, or may instead be approached from B♭ or G, creating a Phrygian cadence.

10. Use ¢ as meter signature and use bar lines. Begin the melody on beat one, and end either with a whole note on beat three tied to a breve, or a breve on beat one. The sense of secondary rhythm derived from the prose rhythm should offset a tendency regularly to stress the first beat of the measure. Sing the completed melody. If it is difficult to sing, there is probably a reason that can be identified in one of the above precepts.

Examine the following melodies for rhythm, text setting, balance of stepwise movement and leaps, and cadence approach. Sing them, noticing the ease with which they can be performed.

Example 4-4

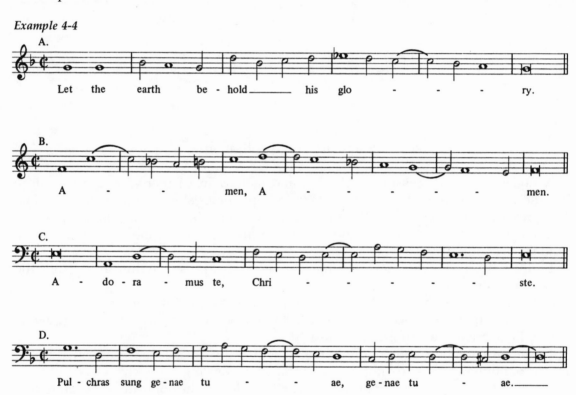

Exercises

1. Using the following texts, and taking into consideration the preceding discussion, compose melodies in different modes and for different voice parts. Indicate the voice parts and the mode, and use correct notational procedures with stems correctly turned and spaced on the staff.

1. Laudate nomen Domini.
   (Praise the name of the Lord.)

2. Afferte Domino gloriam et honorem.
   (Ascribe unto the Lord glory and honor.)

3. In domum Domini ibimus.
   (Let us go to the house of the Lord.)

2. Sing the melodies you have written, analyzing the cause of any awkward or difficult-to-sing areas. Make adjustments or corrections to improve the presentation of the text, naturalness for the voices, and rhythmic variety.

5
Beginning Two-Voice Counterpoint

Vertical Intervallic Relationships

When two or more melodic lines are combined, the result is called counterpoint. In the sixteenth century the combined lines of melody obeyed principles for intervallic relationships that were clearly established and respected. While most of the writing was for more than two voices, composers sometimes wrote sets of pieces for two voices or instruments, often call *bicinia*, and also included two-voice sections in works predominantly for more voices. The duos in Lasso's setting of the *Penitential Psalms* are representative of such two-voice compositions.

Intervallic relationships between voices are always calculated from the lowest pitch. Since voices may cross at times, the normally higher voice briefly becoming the lower, the interval is considered from the lowest-sounding note, not in terms of the lowest-named voice part. Intervals are categorized as consonances, which can move freely, and dissonances, which can be used only within carefully prescribed circumstances. The consonant intervals in the style are the unison, octave, perfect fifth, major and minor third, major and minor sixth. Dissonant intervals include the second, fourth, seventh, and all diminished and augmented intervals.

Two-part counterpoint is generally written for the same or adjacent voices, tenor and bass for example, with the melodic lines seldom more than an octave apart. Instances of wider spacing are often the result of imitation of theme or interpretation of text. Likewise, infrequent crossing of voices may be the result of imitation or interpretation of text. Such variations in voice-part relationships, used sparingly, add interest to the texture.

Cadence

The cadence, both interior and final, consists of an octave or unison approached by step from above and below. Called the *clausula vera* (true close), the cadence in the Dorian, Lydian, Mixolydian, Aeolian, and Ionian has an ascending half step and a descending whole step into the final note, with musica ficta creating the ascending half step when needed. The Phrygian cadence requires no accidental; it has a descending half step and an ascending whole step into the final, the reverse cadence approach from that of the other modes. Observe in the cadences of example 5-1 that a minor third moves to a unison, a major sixth to an octave.

Example 5-1

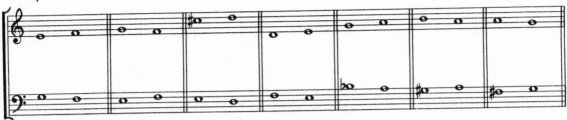

Contour and Linear Movement

The individual melodic lines of a contrapuntal composition constitute the horizontal aspect of its texture, while the intervals occurring between the melodic lines create the vertical aspect. The addition of a rhythmic design for each melody, free yet coordinated under established principles for the whole structure, completes the sense of linear interaction, of give and take in contrapuntal music. Although the intervallic structures are largely consonant, the introduction of dissonance with its ability to interrupt rhythmic flow adds to the unpredictable variety of the style.

In the beginning writing of two-voice counterpoint, the rhythmic resources will be limited to breves, whole notes and half notes, as in the beginning melody writing. The different treatment of the various note values can best be considered after the style has been examined further. Preparatory to the combining of melodic lines, these basic factors should be considered:

1. The range of each voice part limits the melodic resources; in order that the identity of the lines be retained, voice crossing should be kept to a minimum.

2. Unisons and octaves on beat one or three are generally used at the beginnings and endings of phrases. (This will change with the addition of quarter notes). On beat two or four they should be approached and left by contrary or oblique motion. In rare instances the octave is found on beat one or three, but the sound is weakening and is best avoided. See example 5-2A.

3. The perfect fifth between voices is usually approached by contrary or oblique motion. Rarely, the fifth is approached in similar motion, one voice by step, the other by leap, as in example 5-2B.

4. Consecutive perfect fifths and octaves are not in the style (see example 5-2C). Patterns of fifths in similar motion with imperfect consonances intervening are possible, as shown in example 5-2D.

Example 5-2

avoid

5. Thirds and sixths may be approached and left freely, but more than three in succession when longer note values are used tend to destroy the independence of the individual melodic lines.

6. Voice parts are written on separate staves, with text underlay for each part. Contrary motion between parts allows more opportunity for individual melodic contour to be heard, but oblique motion also gives opportunity for individuality in the rhythmic variation brought about by a voice remaining stationary while the other voice moves. Similar motion, with its tendency to inhibit individual melodic contour, should be used sparingly.

7. The cadence should be the clausula vera, with its whole- and half-step movement into the doubled final, and no raised notes are used in the Phrygian cadence on E or in the transposed Phrygian on A. (B♭ descends to A).

Observe the following examples of two-voice writing for their individual melodic qualities and their contrapuntal relationships. The upper voice of example 5-3A becomes the lower voice in example 5-3B.

Example 5-3

EXERCISE

Compose in white notes a melodic setting of each of the following text fragments, selecting a different mode and voice part for each melody and concluding on the final. Using the melody as upper voice, write a counterpoint below it; then, placing the melody in the lower voice write a counterpoint above it. Use only consonant intervals and arrive at a clausula vera on the final of the mode. Use adjacent voices, or write for two of the same part. Sing the parts individually and make changes where awkwardness is felt.

1. Benedictus qui venit.

2. Adoramus te, Christe.

3. Laudate Dominum.

Dissonance

While consonance was the basis of the sixteenth-century harmonic sound, it was discord as it interrupted concord that provided the stimulus for a return to consonance. The dissonances were introduced and left by established rules, one of which required that there be a stepwise approach to the dissonance. Another established procedure required the dissonance to be left by step, the only exception being the *nota cambiata*, to be discussed in chapter 6.

In accordance with the pedagogical approach of beginning with simpler writing in white notes before proceeding to more complex writing involving beat subdivision, the dissonance examined will be those forms that require an entire beat: namely, the half-note passing tone and the suspension. All other dissonance involves subdividing the beat.

The half-note passing tone occurs on beat two or four, the so-called weak beats, and the suspension occurs on beat one or three. The design of primary and secondary rhythm is felt in these two devices, for the passing tone occurs over a sustained note initiated on the preceding beat, creating a mild effect of discord. The suspension, on the other hand, is a dissonance that is intended to disturb or to jar both the linear and the intervallic movement. Consonance, after the suspension, has an effect of inevitable reasonableness. The suspension is identified with strong beats, the passing tone with weak beats.

The half-note passing tone may occur ascending or descending on beat two or four, and like any passing tone, is a note approached and left stepwise without change of direction. It may be above or below a sustaining voice, which itself may be approached or left by leap provided it is in place at least one beat before the dissonant note appears and sustained until the dissonance is completed. The half-note passing tone, therefore, cannot be attempted in relation to a note whose length, initiated on the preceding beat, is less than a whole note. This principle does not change with the addition of black notation. The dissonant interval between the two voices may be a second, fourth, seventh, tritone, or a compound equivalent.

The following measures, one through four, illustrate passing tones correctly used. Measures five through eight contain errors, the analysis of which should help to clarify the restrictions for controlling the use of the half-note passing tone.

Example 5-4

EXERCISE

Observe the Mixolydian melody (example 5-5) containing half notes approached and left by step, which could, in combination with another voice, become passing tones. Using the melody as the cantus firmus, write a counterpoint below it, and for further practice, place the cantus firmus in the lower part and write a counterpoint above it. An awareness of primary and secondary rhythm remains an essential consideration and is not superseded by the expansion of other resources.

Example 5-5

The suspension is a note that becomes dissonant when delayed in its descending stepwise movement, the dissonance occurring on beat one or three. The suspension is a more obvious dissonance than the passing tone, not only because of the beat on which it occurs, but because the delaying of the note, sounding as a consonance at least one beat before it becomes a dissonance, tends to focus attention on the note. The note that is to be delayed is referred to as the preparation note, and it appears on beat two or four as a consonance. It is then sustained into the following beat one or three and becomes the suspension itself, for as it sustains its pitch the other voice moves, causing the sustained note to become dissonant. The dissonant note then moves downward by step on the next beat to a consonant resolution note. The suspension device always consists of three parts: preparation, suspension, resolution. The preparation note that appears on beat four may be tied across the bar line to a half note. Without bar lines, the sixteenth-century scribe wrote the preparation and the suspension as one long note; with present-day bar lines the suspension on beat three is a continuation of a whole note initiated on beat two or of a dotted whole note on beat one. The setting of the text reflected the assumption that the preparation and the suspension were one note, and the pitch on the suspended beat rarely accommodated a second syllable of text.

Suspensions are named in relation to the dissonant note and its consonant resolution. The 7–6 and the 2–3 are the most effective in two voices, particularly at the cadence, in that the sixth moves into the octave and the third into the unison. The resolution note is the leading tone. The 4–3 suspension is effective within the phrase, and in more than two voices is useful cadentially. The 9–8 and 2–1 suspensions are undesirable in two voices in that they resolve into the empty octave or unison, with any sense of delay offset by the fact that the resolution note is already present in the other voice. Illustrations of suspensions may be seen in Example 5–6.

Example 5-6

7 - 6   2 - 3   4 - 3   9 - 8   7   2 - 3   7 - 6

Notice in the above illustration that the 2–3 is the only suspension in the lower voice. For all suspensions, the three-part structure consists of:

1. Preparation—consonance on beat two or four;
2. Suspension—dissonance on beat one or three;
3. Resolution—consonance on beat two or four; approached by descending step.

EXERCISES

1. Each of the "suspensions" in example 5-7 is incorrectly written. What is the error in each instance?

Example 5-7

2. Sing the following two-voice examples, observing both visually and aurally the suspensions and the half-note passing tones.

Example 5-8

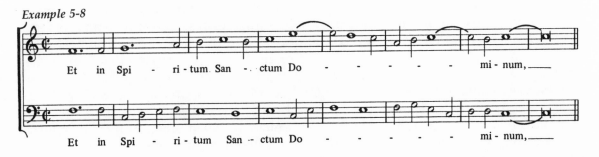

Et in Spi - ri - tum San - ctum Do - - - - mi - num, ___

Et in Spi - ri - tum San - ctum Do - - - - mi - num, ___

San - ctus, ___ San - - - ctus, San - ctus. ___

San - ctus, San - - - ctus, San - - ctus. ___

3. Employing the melody in example 5-9 as lower voice, write a counterpoint in white notes that includes suspensions and half-note passing tones. There must be a suspension delaying the leading tone (or simply the seventh modal degree in the Phrygian mode) which moves into the final. Apply musica ficta where needed.

Example 5-9

4. Using an approach of three measures, write a phrase in each mode concluding with a 7–6 or 2–3 suspension at the cadence, as in the example below.

Example 5-10

Imitation

The entry of parts at different times using the same thematic material is the general definition of imitation. The imitating voices may state the theme beginning on a different pitch from the first voice; however, the intervallic distances most often used between voices are the fifth, the octave or unison, and the fourth. When the imitating voice enters close to the beginning of the first voice, the imitation is said to be in *stretto*.

Contrapuntal music makes extensive use of imitation. The reuse of theme creates a feeling of unity, an intriguing interweaving of material that contributes to the characteristic richness of sound in the polyphonic music of the sixteenth century. Where later music was organized around an established principle of root movement toward the tonic key center, the sixteenth-century music with its varied modes, its free rhythmic design, and uneven phrase length achieved a strong feeling of unity through imitation of thematic material. The text underlay of the original melody was also repeated in the imitation and contributed to the recognition of the subject as it was restated in other voices. Generally the imitating voice entered on a beat comparable to the entry of the first voice; that is, beat one might be imitated by beat one or beat three.

Imitation is strict, free, tonal, or real. Strict imitation, called canon, is the oldest form of imitation, dating from the thirteenth century. Its initial theme is referred to as the leader *(Dux)*, and the imitation as the follower *(Comes)*. The imitation in canon is note for note, although not interval for interval, as, for example, when the imitation starting on the fifth above the initial note encounters a minor third where the original melody has a major third. The imitation is still considered canonic if a major interval is imitated by a minor interval and a minor interval by a major interval. Perfect intervals, however, are imitated only by perfect intervals. Canon is sometimes interrupted rhythmically and intervallically in order to achieve a cadence. This is done no sooner than the penultimate measure. Sing the example below, noticing the treatment of the canon at the cadence. The quarter notes in this and the following examples should not be confusing in that the present writing in longer time-values will naturally be followed by the other values, beginning with the next chapter.

Example 5-11
Victoria: *Passio secundum Matthaeum*

Examine also *Penitential Psalms*, VII, verse 6 (p. 245). The imitation is canonic through measure ten, with slight changes in measures eleven and twelve, continuing in free imitation to the final cadence in measure seventeen. A further example of canon may be seen in Psalm VI, verse 2 (p. 222), where the alto and tenor have the psalm tone in canon at the fifth.

In free imitation the second voice imitates only the beginning notes of the first voice and continues without imitation to a cadence point (example 5-12). After the cadence there is likely to be a free imitation of the next subject introduced, and a continuation in free counterpoint.

Example 5-12
Lasso: *Conditor alme siderum* (hymn)

See also *Penitential Psalms*, V, verse 2 (p. 170). The imitation is at the unison, with only the opening arpeggio repeated in the second entry.

The terms *tonal* and *real* are more applicable to later music and its fugal writing than to the sixteenth-century music. In tonal imitation an adjustment is made to enable the imitating voice to retain the tonic-dominant relationship established in the opening theme. In a real imitation the second voice imitates the first without intervallic change. Sixteenth-century composers preferred the real imitation.

In Example 5-13 the opening fifth is imitated by a fifth.

Example 5-13
Palestrina: Benedictus *(Missa Gabriel archangelus)*

Tonal imitation may be seen in *Penitential Psalms*, III, verse 23 (p. 125). The first four voice entries reveal an alternation between the leaps E–A and A–E.

Imitation can be varied further by the use of the following devices, applicable to both canonic and free imitation:

1. *Inversion* (mirroring) is the imitation of the intervals of the subject in contrary motion. In the example below, notice the ascending fifth imitated by a descending fifth.

Example 5-14
Palestrina: *Surrexit pastor bonus* (motet)

Additional examples may be found in *Penitential Psalms*, IV, verse 12 (p. 149), in which each point of imitation begins on A and inverts the intervals of the preceding entry; and in Psalm V, verse 19 (p. 197) the imitating voice is at the fourth, and two consecutive motives are mirrored.

2. *Augmentation* is imitation in which the original note-values of the theme are doubled (or tripled or quadrupled).

Example 5-15
Victoria: Credo *(Missa Ave maris stella)*

3. *Diminution* is imitation in which the original note-values of the theme are halved. It is rarely used beyond the first few notes.

Example 5-16
Palestrina: Kyrie *(Missa brevis)*

4. *Cancrizans* (crab) is canon in which the imitating voice reverses the notes of the leader. It was rarely used in the sixteenth century.

By the middle of the sixteenth century the use of canonic techniques had declined.

Short sections of canonic writing within a larger work, or canon in two voices within a framework of free imitation in other voices, continued to be fairly common.

EXERCISES

A beginning plan for writing imitation, starting with free imitation, might be as follows:

Write the first notes of the leader; at a selected point have the follower enter, copying the leader a fifth above or below, at which time new counterpoint will be composed in the lead voice that will next be used in the following voice. Both voices then proceed in free counterpoint to a cadence appropriate to the mode. The diagram below shows the plan, and the following phrase illustrates its realization in a free imitation at the fifth, written in the Dorian mode, cadencing on the final.

Follower_____counterpoint........................

                                                                    cadence

      Leader_____counterpoint........................

Example 5-17

Using the suggested plan, compose a two-voice imitative setting of each of the following text fragments of around six measures in length, varying the devices of imitation as specified. Write for different voices; use different modes; vary the interval of imitation; use half-note passing tones and suspensions within the phrase, and always use a suspension into the leading tone of the penultimate chord at the cadence. Secondary rhythm must be employed; movement in one voice against stationary notes in the other voice is vital to contrapuntal rhythm.

1. Hosanna in excelsis (mirrored imitation).

2. Alleluia (canon).

3. Amen (augmentation).

4. Sanctus, sanctus, sanctus (free imitation).

6
Melody Writing with All Note Values

Quarter Notes in Stepwise Succession

Stepwise movement in quarter notes is far more frequent than leaps. There are additional considerations of rhythm and dissonance that apply to quarter notes because of their subdivision of the beat.

Quarter notes are more often found in stepwise motion without change of direction. A dotted half note may precede a single quarter note. Interior phrases may begin with quarter notes, but the beginning note of a composition is no shorter than a dotted half note. The quarter-note rest is rare.

Example 6-1
Lasso: Benedictus *(Missa Puis que i'ay perdu)*

Scalewise pairs of quarter notes may occur on beats two or four. Following a half note they may either ascend or descend, but after a whole note or dotted note they usually descend.

Example 6-2
Palestrina: Gloria *(Missa In te Domine speravi)*   Ibid.

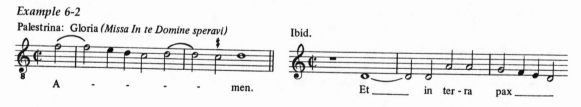

Stepwise pairs of quarter notes without change of direction occur infrequently on beats one or three and are usually encountered leading to the preparation of a suspension.

Example 6-3
Palestrina: Credo *(Missa Sine nomine)*

Stepwise quarter-note passages may change direction on the first part of a beat from below or from above. Changing direction on the second half of a beat creates the effect of upper and lower auxiliary notes. The lower auxiliary is more common to the style than the upper. The infrequency of the upper auxiliary relates largely to instances where quarter notes follow the upper auxiliary. An upper auxiliary followed by a half note or a still longer note is not infrequent.

Example 6-4
Lasso: Kyrie *(Missa de feria)*   Ibid.   Ibid.

Sequential passages of quarter notes are rare in the style, as is redundancy of any kind in the melodic line. Two examples of sequence are quoted below:

Example 6-5
Lasso: *Penitential Psalms*, VII, verse 6   Palestrina: Sanctus *(Missa Ut, re, mi, fa, sol, la)*

Quarter Notes and Leaps

An approach by leap to a quarter-note passage from white notes is generally made from a half note. The leap is made ascending or descending, and after the leap there is a change of direction. When a passage of stepwise quarter notes is left by leap, the leap is always made in the opposite direction to the movement of the quarter-note passage.

Example 6-6
Palestrina: Kyrie *(Missa L'homme armé)*   Victoria: *Magnificat tertii toni*

Within quarter-note passages with change of direction, leaps are made ascending and descending into the first half of a beat. Leaps into the second half of a beat are nearly always descending. An ascending leap into the second half of a beat creates an illusion of accent, an offbeat syncopation within one voice that lacks the subtlety of the secondary rhythm of the style. However, there are uses of such syncopation; a particularly colorful instance is in the *Penitential Psalms*, II, verse 11 (p. 65) where Lasso, in setting the text, "Nolite fieri sicut equus et mulus," uses awkward melodic and rhythmic confusion, including an ascending leap into the second half of a beat to suggest the uncomprehending nature of the mule.

A descending leap into the second half of a beat is generally followed by ascending movement by step or by leap (example 6-7A). When the descending leap is no larger than a third, the melody may continue in the same downward direction as the leap. A descending leap may be made from a dotted half note, after which the direction must change. Two consecutive leaps in the same direction in quarter notes are rare, although in longer note-values a triad is frequently arpeggiated. A dotted half note (the dot representing a quarter note) is not followed by two descending leaps in quarter notes. However, change of direction following the first leap is often made by leap, as seen in example 6-7B.

Example 6-7
Palestrina: Gloria *(Missa O Regem coeli)*   Victoria: *Quam pulchri sunt gressus tui* (motet)

The leap of an octave may precede or follow another leap provided the direction of the second leap changes. In example 6-8 a descending third is followed by an ascending octave, a descending fifth is followed by an ascending octave, and a descending octave is followed by an ascending fifth.

Example 6-8
Morales: *Magnificat tertii toni*   Lasso: Credo *(Missa Surge propera)*

A favorite melodic idiom of the sixteenth century is the *nota cambiata* (or changed note). The four-note figure consists of a descending step followed by a descending leap of a third which then ascends a step, as though filling in the leap. In earlier times the structure of the figure was varied, sometimes consisting of three notes, and even in the beginning of the sixteenth century the device is used by Josquin with the fourth note approached by descending leap.* However, the form indicated in example 6-9, with rhythmic variations as shown, is the form employed almost exclusively after the early part of the century.

Example 6-9

When the cambiata figure begins on beat two or four it is frequently approached by an ascending pair of quarter notes on preceding beat one or three, as in a similar approach to the preparation of a suspension (example 6-10).

Example 6-10
Palestrina: Agnus Dei *(Missa Sanctorum meritis)*   Ibid.   Victoria: *O decus apostolicum* (motet)

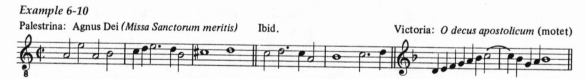

The cambiata may be initiated on any beat, and is often found at the approach to a final cadence, its fourth note becoming the third of the final chord, with an accidental added where needed to create a major third.

Example 6-11
Palestrina: Agnus Dei *(Missa Pater noster)*   Palestrina: Gloria *(Missa De Beata Virgine)*

A single quarter note approached by step from above and repeated is called a *portamento,* or anticipation. It is found on the second half of beat one or three, and is

---

*Jeppesen, *The Style of Palestrina and the Dissonance,* p. 210.

repeated on the following beat. The portamento may forecast a white note or another quarter note. It is most often used as a part of a suspension ornament, taking the second half of the suspension beat to anticipate the resolution note.

Example 6-12
Victoria: *Magi viderunt stellam* (motet)

Eighth Notes

Eighth notes are found as stepwise pairs on the second half of any beat. They are approached and left by step, preceded by a dotted half note or a quarter note. An interval of a fourth, ascending or descending, may be filled in with two eighth notes (Example 6-13A).

Change of direction in the melodic line may occur on either of the two eighth notes, creating an auxiliary note. The lower auxiliary is encountered more frequently than the upper (example 6-13B). A pair of eighth notes often embellishes the resolution of a suspension. In example 6-13C may be seen a suspension figure in augmentation, a pair of quarter notes on beat two embellishing the resolution to the whole note on beat three. Following it is another example of a suspension embellished by eighth notes.

Example 6-13
Palestrina: Kyrie *(Missa Emendemus)*   Lasso: Credo *(Missa Beatus qui intelligit)*

The style incorporates eighth-note pairs largely as embellishments, and exceptions to the stepwise approach and departure are infrequent, generally occurring when a descending pair preceded by a dotted half note is left by ascending leap to return to the note that preceded it (example 6-14A). Exceptions to the placement of eighth notes on the offbeat are rare, and consecutive eighth-note pairs are likewise seldom found. One such instance may be seen in example 6-14B. An octave D–D, divided at G into a fourth and a fifth, has the fifth filled in by four eighth notes. Their movement ends on a suspension preparation.

Example 6-14
Palestrina: *Veni, Domine* (motet)   Palestrina: Gloria *(Missa Emendemus)*

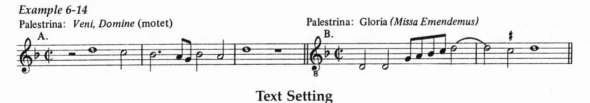

Text Setting

Prose rhythm with its irregular succession of stressed and unstressed syllables is reflected in the agogic accents of the sixteenth-century vocal polyphony. The principles of text underlay had developed gradually, and, enunciated by the theorist Zarlino, were widely followed.* An examination of the textual treatment reveals the following:

---

*Gioseffo Zarlino, *Le Istitutioni harmoniche*, Part 4 (1558), trans. Vered Cohen, ed. Claude V. Palisca (New Haven: Yale University Press, 1983), pp. 97–99.

1. The accentuation of the Latin text generally coincides with the musical stresses. The means of stress include length of note, approach by leap, metric placement, and height of pitch.

2. The first syllable of text is placed on the long note with which the composition begins, without consideration for its normal stressed or unstressed role. Likewise, the final syllable of text is placed with the last note, a breve or longer, regardless of the normal length or stress of the final syllable of the word. However, within the composition those same syllables are treated differently if their normal enunciation interprets them as short and unstressed.

3. Generally all white notes may each carry a syllable. A single quarter note does not carry a syllable except when following a dotted half note. The quarter note bears only a short syllable, as shown in example 6-15A.

4. The first note of a passage of quarter notes that begins on a beat may carry a syllable of text, but no syllabic change should occur within the passage. An interior phrase beginning with quarter notes (not less than four) will carry a syllable of text (example 6-15B).

Example 6-15
Lasso: Credo *(Missa Congratulamini mihi)*

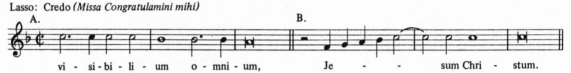

5. The syllable will not change on the first white note following a passage of quarter notes. The quarter-note passage is concluded on a white note, and the syllable is changed on the next note. In performance the sound is smoother when the momentum of the quarter-note passage and the text are not changed simultaneously (example 6-16A).

6. Eighth notes do not carry a syllable, nor is there a change of syllable on the note following the eighths (example 6-16B).

Example 6-16
Lasso: Credo *(Missa Congratulamini mihi)*

7. Generally the text setting is planned so that the final note of a section is not preceded by a quarter note carrying the penultimate syllable. However, in instances where the quarter note must carry the penultimate syllable, the text change may occur after the quarter note to enable the last long note to have the final syllable (example 6-17A). Rarely, the last note is repeated, enabling the syllable to change on the repeated note, as in example 6-17B.

Example 6-17
Palestrina: *(In Communiunius Martyris* (hymn)   Palestrina: *Laudate pueri* (motet)

8. The textual treatment of the first voice must be repeated in all voices that imitate it.

9. Repeated notes that are not in the nature of ornamentation require syllabic change. The *portamento,* as in example 6-18, does not require a change of syllable.

Example 6-18
Lasso: Credo *(Missa Congratulamini mihi)*

Scri - ptu - - - - - - - - ras.

All of the material addressed in the preceding discussions is in preparation for writing melody, melody that reflects the character and prose rhythm of a text within the style of sixteenth-century vocal polyphony. A review should be made of the initial notes and cadence points for each mode. Other features of importance may be reviewed by examining the following texted melody, which contains errors in text setting and in melody writing.

Example 6-19
Mode III

Glo - - ri - a _____ in ex - cel - sis De - - o.

EXERCISE

Compose a melodic setting of each of the following texts, or set a text of your own choosing. The meter signature is to be 4/2 and all note-values are to be used. Indicate the voice part and the mode. Read each text aloud, observing the syllables that are stressed, the short syllables, and the general character of the text. Represent the prose rhythm by employing the subtleties of agogic accent. Sing the completed melody, reconstructing it where awkwardness is felt.

1. Come, O Lord, and do not delay.

2. Benedictus qui venit in nomine Domini.

3. Hosanna in excelsis.

4. Be still and know that I am God.

An example, using the English text, "In thee, O Lord, do I trust," is given below.

Example 6-20

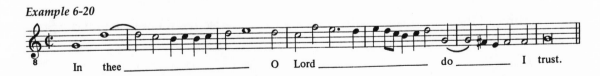

In thee _____ O Lord _____ do _____ I trust.

Singing, hearing, and analyzing the procedures employed in representative works can greatly increase the understanding of the style. While editions that retain the half note as the unit of beat represent the white notation of the manuscript sources, modern editions, which for practical reasons use the quarter note as the unit of beat, are frequently more available to the student. Yet transcriptions of the historical ₵ into the modern 4/4 can be confusing to one whose knowledge of the style is tied to the study of the music in white notation only and to whom the use of the quarter note as the beat is disturbing; for in the transcriptions the quarter note replaces the half note and previous restrictions on the use of quarter notes are now transferred to eighth notes.

Therefore, it is of value, early in the study of the style, to relate the historic white notation to black notation, to experience the conversion of the note-values by making transcriptions, to become accustomed, through frequent encounters, to the elements of the style as they may be expressed in another equally precise rhythmic notational system. For a gradual adjustment to the dual task of developing an understanding of the aspects of the style and recognizing its representation in modern notation, it is suggested that singing be done in both notations and that observations be made on the conversion of the note-values and the constancy of the rhythmic relationships. In the following examples the meter signature ₵ is rendered first in 4/2 meter, then in 4/4. Analyze and compare the versions, observing the text setting in light of the features recently discussed, the use of offbeat rhythmic movement, leaps involving the offbeat, and devices such as portamento.

Example 6-21

Lasso: Agnus Dei *(Missa Locutus sum)*

EXERCISE

Select three of the previously written melodies and transcribe them in 4/4 meter. Sing both versions.

7
Two-Voice Counterpoint with All Note Values

General Observations

Two-voice compositions of sixteenth-century composers are the obvious source for the study of the techniques of two-voice writing. However, compositions for three or more voices were so constructed that each upper part formed correct two-voice counterpoint in relation to the lowest part. Therefore, one can learn much about the techniques of handling two voices through the study of the much larger repertory of music for three or more voices.

In this chapter the procedures for writing two-voice counterpoint discussed previously will be continued, and the use of quarter notes and eighth notes in two-voice texture will be considered

Treatment of Dissonance

PASSING TONES

The passing tone, a dissonance approached and left by step without change of direction, is generally dissonant against a note in another voice that is double or more its length. An unaccented quarter-note passing tone is one that is employed on the second half of any beat, ascending or descending, while an accented quarter-note passing tone occurs only on the first half of beat two or four, restricted to a descending melodic line. The descending movement of the dissonant note to its offbeat resolution note parallels in shorter time duration the movement of the suspension from the strong beat to its resolution on the weak beat.

Example 7-1
Lasso: Credo *(Missa Doulce memoire)*

With stepwise approach, the first note of a pair of quarter notes may be an accented passing tone, the second note being consonant and left by ascending leap, as in example 7-2A. Four quarter notes descending stepwise from beat one or three, the first two of which are consonant and the third dissonant, are left by ascending step after the fourth note. Their resemblance to the cambiata figure requires the turn of the melody, as seen in example 7-2B. Generally, any stepwise passage of quarter notes that includes an accented passing tone will change direction after the dissonant note has descended into its offbeat resolution.

Example 7-2
Palestrina: Gloria *(Missa Vestiva i colli)*

AUXILIARY NOTES

The auxiliary, or neighboring tone, occurs on the second half of any beat, ascending or descending. Its stepwise design of leaving and returning to the same pitch frequently employs only consonance. As a dissonance, the upper neighbor is far less frequent than the lower; when used it usually returns to a note longer than a quarter note (example 7-3A).

Eighth notes, employed in pairs on the second half of the beat, may be consonant, or may be passing tones or auxiliary notes. They are frequently an ornament to the resolution of a suspension, the first eighth note a portamento, the second an auxiliary note to the portamento. Eighth notes are usually approached from above (example 7-3B).

Example 7-3
Palestrina: *O sancte praesul Nicolae* (motet)

PORTAMENTOS

The portamento, or anticipation, occurs on the second half of beat one or three. It may be consonant or dissonant, and is approached by descending step. The consonant portamento frequently occurs with the suspension, appearing on the second half of the suspension beat forecasting the resolution note on the following beat. The suspension in a concluding cadence is usually not ornamented by a quarter-note portamento but is embellished instead by a pair of eighth notes. Variations in the use of the consonant portamento in combination with quarter notes and eighth-note pairs may be seen in example 7-4.

Example 7-4
Lasso: *Cantiones duarum vocum,* No. 5   Ibid., No. 8

The portamento may be used as a melodic device with no suspension involved. It may be consonant, but unlike the movement from a suspension, it can also be preceded by consonance and itself be dissonant. Although the portamento may be consonant or dissonant and may be preceded by a suspension or not, these features are rarely varied: (1) it is approached by descending step; (2) it occurs on the second half of beat one or three.

CAMBIATAS

In the nota cambiata, the first and third notes must be consonant; the second and fourth notes may be consonant or dissonant. The first note, even when a dotted half note, must be consonant its full length, no dissonance arriving with the dot. The second note of the cambiata is the only dissonance in the style involving a leap. The third note, regardless of its length, is consonant. The fourth note may be dissonant, provided it is so placed as to be treated as a passing tone. In Example 7-5 may be seen the cambiata in different rhythms. Notice also the dissonant portamento.

Example 7-5
Victoria: *Magnificat quarti toni*   Ibid.

SUSPENSIONS

The suspension, appearing on beat one or three, is the strongest dissonance in the style. It serves a braking function in its delay of the leading tone near the cadence and adds drama and impetus for movement into consonance wherever it is placed. There are devices for varying it that add to the interest it generates. There may be an accented passing tone in relation to the preparation note, as seen in example 7-6A. The bass may change to another consonant note at the time of resolution (example 7-6B). There is often an ornamentation of the suspended note using a quarter-note anticipation or a pair of eighth notes consisting of an anticipation and its lower neighbor (example 7-6C). The suspension, the ornament, and the resolution may be in augmentation, requiring four or more beats instead of two, as shown in example 7-6D. The suspension in augmentation is most often used in the final cadence.

Example 7-6

Lasso: Sanctus *(Missa Laudate Dominum)*   Lasso: Kyrie *(Missa Locutus sum)*

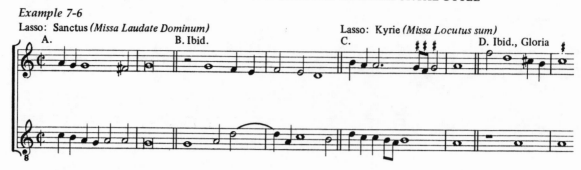

A.   B. Ibid.   C.   D. Ibid., Gloria

The following summary of the placement of dissonance should be studied before further writing is undertaken. Since consonance may be used on any beat or subdivision of a beat, only the placement of dissonance is listed.

Placement of Dissonance

ON BEATS 1 AND 3

Suspensions, all types

ON SECOND HALF OF BEATS 1 AND 3

Unaccented passing tones, ascending and
    descending and descending portamento
Second tone of nota cambiata
Lower and upper auxiliary notes

ON BEATS 2 AND 4

Half-note passing tones, ascending
    and descending
Accented quarter-note passing tones,
    descending

ON SECOND HALF OF BEATS 2 AND 4

All dissonance listed on the second half of
    beats 1 and 3 except portamento

Example 7-7 contains errors in melodic movement, dissonance, rhythm, and contrapuntal relationships. Some of the errors are easily identified; others will be apparent only after spacing, voice leading, and overall handling of dissonance are considered. The instructor will find it profitable to provide other similar exercises as the study progresses.

Example 7-7

EXERCISES

1. Write a counterpoint, without imitation, above or below the following melody. Try to include, for the sake of practice in writing them, as many of the devices of dissonance as can be correctly accommodated.

Example 7-8

2. Using the given text, or one of your own choosing, write a nonimitative piece of about ten measures in which you incorporate:

    a) *nota cambiata*
    b) ornamented suspension
    c) dissonant portamento
    d) accented passing tone
    e) neighboring tone

Text: Great peace have they which love thy law.

Imitation

While imitations are more often at the fourth or the fifth, they can be found at all perfect, major, or minor intervals. Imitation between voices of equal range is likely to be at the unison, second, or third. The mode may be indicated by having the voices enter alternately on the final and the dominant. However, cadence points and melodic movement may also suggest the mode. Free imitation is most often used, with variety provided by mirror, augmentation, and infrequently, diminution. Strict imitation, canon, is infrequent for an entire piece in two voices, although shorter sections of canon are often included.

EXERCISES

Using the given subject head, write:

1. Free imitation at the fifth, continuing in free counterpoint for six to eight measures to an appropriate cadence point. Use the contrapuntal resources studied, and precede the final cadence with a 7–6 or 2–3 ornamented suspension.

2. A mirrored imitation, completing as stipulated above.

3. A canon, continuing for four measures to a cadence.

4. A transcription of the subject in 4/4 meter, imitating at the unison and continuing in free counterpoint to a cadence.

Example 7-9

Double Counterpoint

Double counterpoint, or invertible counterpoint, is a contrapuntal texture so designed that the parts may be exchanged, the upper becoming the lower, and the lower becoming the upper. If the method is applied to three parts, it is called triple counterpoint, to four parts, quadruple counterpoint. Although it is a textural device often encountered in Baroque fugal technique, it is used sparingly by sixteenth-century composers.

The intervals of inversion most often encountered are those of the octave, tenth, and twelfth. The inversion at the twelfth is favored by Renaissance composers.

In double counterpoint at the octave one part remains stationary while the other moves up or down an octave, across the other part. The result of this inversion is that the octave between the voices in the original becomes a unison, a seventh becomes a second, and so on. The table of inversion given below shows the original intervals between the parts and their inversions.

INVERSION AT THE OCTAVE

Original intervals	1	2	3	4	5	6	7	8
become in inversion	8	7	6	5	4	3	2	1

All intervals remain of the same type, except for the fifth, which becomes a fourth and therefore a dissonance. In the original counterpoint the fifth must be so placed that when inverted it becomes a half-note or quarter-note passing tone, suspension, or other dissonance of the style on the proper beat. The 7–6, 2–3, and 4–3 suspensions may be used. Inversion at the octave is not achieved if the distance between the original parts exceeds an octave. If melodic movement makes it desirable to exceed an octave or to cross voices, the interval will then remain uninverted. Notice in example 7-10 the voice crossing in measure 2. When one voice of the original counterpoint is moved an octave, the third is not inverted but becomes a tenth. Observe also the inversion of the fifth to become a correctly executed suspension, and another fifth that becomes a passing tone.

Example 7-10

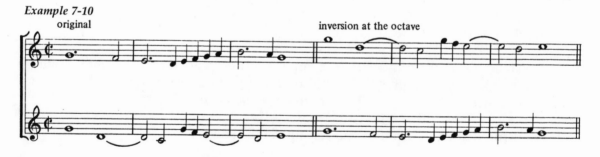

As can be seen from the table of inversion, each original interval and its inversion add to nine. If when a voice is moved an octave the range becomes too high or too low, the two voices may be transposed and inverted simultaneously by moving each voice any combination of intervals whose sum is nine. For example, the upper voice may move down a fourth and the lower voice up a fifth, as in example 7-11. Observe the change in mode brought about by inverting in this manner.

Example 7-11

In the following passage from Palestrina, the inversion is at the octave, the upper voice upon inversion becoming the bass.

Example 7-12
Palestrina: Credo *(Missa Iste Confessor)*

Counterpoint invertible at the fifteenth, two octaves, is in principle the same as inversion at the octave. The inversion is usually accompanied by transposition.

Double counterpoint at the tenth is infrequent. The table of inversion makes apparent the major problems in writing this inversion. The third inverts to an octave, and the sixth to a fifth. Therefore, in the original counterpoint, consecutive thirds and sixths cannot be used. The only suspension that can be used is the 2–3. It is usually necessary to change the texture to free counterpoint on approaching a cadence.

INVERSION AT THE TENTH

Original intervals	1	2	3	4	5	6	7	8	9	10
become in inversion	10	9	8	7	6	5	4	3	2	1

Example 7-13

Although double counterpoint at the twelfth is more often found in sixteenth-century writing, it, like other inversions, is rarely continued for a long passage. Composers seemed to prefer short phrases of inversion, quickly modifying the imitation and continuing more freely.

INVERSION AT THE TWELFTH

Original intervals	1	2	3	4	5	6	7	8	9	10	11	12
become in inversion	12	11	10	9	8	7	6	5	4	3	2	1

The interval of the sixth, which inverts to a seventh, becomes a problem in inversion at the twelfth. It must be planned in the original counterpoint to become a correctly placed dissonance when inverted. The 7–6 in the original counterpoint will invert to become 6–7 and can be used provided the original sixth continues down by step, allowing the dissonant inverted interval to become a passing tone. The 2–3 suspension becomes 4–3, and 4–3 becomes 2–3. Examine the original intervals and their inverted counterparts in example 7-14, in which the counterpoint is inverted and transposed by moving the voices an octave and a fifth. Notice the sum of the intervals, 13 (8 + 5), is one more than the stated interval of inversion.

Example 7-14

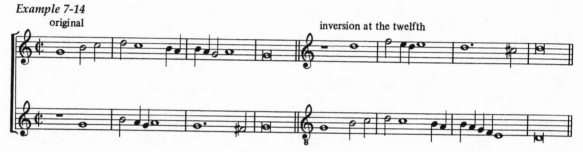

Example 7-15, from Palestrina, illustrates inversion at the twelfth, with the soprano of measures 1–6 dropping a twelfth to become the bass. In measures 10–14, as the alto restates its original pitches, the intervals between the bass and the alto are an inversion at the twelfth of measures 2–6. (The first note of the bass is lengthened.) Notice the sum of the intervals, 13 (12 + 1).

Example 7-15
Palestrina: *Terra tremuit* (offertory)

EXERCISES

1. Write a nonimitative counterpoint invertible at the octave, preparing the fifth to become a properly placed dissonance when inverted. Write an inverted version in which the upper voice drops and the lower voice rises, choosing two intervals whose sum is nine. The necessity of accommodating normal vocal range should influence the choice of intervals for transposition.

2. To the given melody, write a counterpoint at the twelfth for soprano and alto. Invert it by dropping the upper voice an octave and raising the lower voice a fifth.

Example 7-16

3. Examine the previously written counterpoints at the octave and at the twelfth and revise them to become invertible at the tenth.

Formal Structure

Two-voice counterpoint is usually imitative, and as a result, there is little opportunity for chordal treatment. The nature of the text largely determines the structure of the piece. An examination of a sixteenth-century composition reveals that the text is generally divided into short phrases that are introduced and imitated. As each phrase ends in the imitating voice, a new theme is entering in the other voice, overlapping the conclusion of the previous phrase. The overlapping, or dovetailing, technique makes it possible for the melodic flow to continue, as it would not if both voices rested at the same moment. As each theme is imitated, the original text setting is repeated, and the voices, after the imitation is dropped, continue toward a cadence. The same procedure is then repeated for successive phrases, the cadence interrupted each time with the new theme in one voice overlapping the conclusion of the previous phrase in the other voice. This style of through-composition, each interior phrase knit to the preceding phrase, is made more convincing by having the linear emphasis reinforced by the devices of imitation. The final cadence is well defined.

Two versions of the interrupted-cadence structure may be seen in example 7-17. In example 7-17A the *clausula vera* is completed, and while the voice with the leading tone continues, the other voice is interrupted by a rest after which it reenters with a new theme. In the cadence in example 7-17B, the voice with the leading tone continues into the cadence final, while the other voice is interrupted with a rest.

Example 7-17
Lasso: *Penitential Psalms*, IV, verse 9

There are instances when the phrases of text are concluded and separated without the benefit of cadence. They are, however, not concluded with rests simultaneously, and the overlapping phrase endings account for the continuity of sound. The time values of the voices as they end the phrase will vary, but there is no variation in the fact that when there is a suspension present, the voice containing the resolution note will be the one to move to the cadence final.

The opening measure of a composition begins on beat one with a note value no shorter than a dotted half note. Interior phrases, however, may begin with quarter notes and may enter on beat two or four. Themes may be repeated at different intervals, or a theme with its imitation may be heard but once. Interior cadences are generally short, creating little interruption to the rhythmic flow of the music. The structure of the piece reflects the textual subdivision that creates phrases of uneven length and rhythmic design. Examine the *Benedictus* of Lasso; notice the movement from measure 5 to measure 6. The suspension voice completes the cadence, is interrupted, returns with a new theme and text, which after a rest is imitated by the other voice. Notice the repeated phrases, the imitation of each new theme, the syllable given melismatic treatment, the final cadence approach in measure 15 with the anticipation of the preparation note, the accented passing tone, and the 7–6 suspension. Sing the piece, examining it aurally.

Example 7-18
Lasso: **Benedictus** *(Missa Me suffit)*

EXERCISE

Write in free imitation a setting of the following text, overlapping the ending of each phrase with the beginning of the next. The first voice that reenters after a cadence must be imitated by the other voice. Use the clausula vera preceded by a suspension for each cadence, with the final cadence employing an ornamented suspension in augmentation.

Text: Amen, amen, amen.

Two-Voice Compositions for Analysis

Renaissance composers, with the exception of Lasso, wrote little for two voices. Compositions for multiple voices sometimes contained a section for two voices, such as the Benedictus in example 7-18, which is from a four-voice Mass; but only Lasso wrote with any degree of frequency for two voices. There are eight two-voice motets in his setting of the *Penitential Psalms,* and there are other sets of pieces for two voices, notably the *Cantiones duarum vocum.*

The following compositions will serve as additional examples of two-voice texture. Hearing them several times before subsequent analysis will increase their usefulness. They are written for different vocal ranges and may be performed by two voices, or one voice and instrument. The textual treatment should be a part of the analysis, and although having instruments play both parts would clearly present the counterpoint, the text should also be sung. A few comments will precede each composition.

The following brief passage from Victoria is in canon at the unison. As example 7-19 demonstrates, imitation at the unison requires the repeating of pitches within the same range. Voice crossings are frequent, but the lack of tonal variety is difficult to minimize.

Example 7-19

Although the next composition, published by Petrucci in 1502, was written near the close of the fifteenth century, the writing adheres to the general principles of the later sixteenth-century style. Minor differences appear in the placement of dissonance. Notice in measure 8 the dissonant preparation of the suspension, and in measures 13–14 the anticipation arising from a weak beat. Josquin divides the *Benedictus* into three sections, each section a mensuration canon with one voice simply doubling the note values of the other in regular augmentation. The first of the three sections is provided in example 7-20. The meter signature ₵ is rendered in relation to the whole note.

Example 7-20
Josquin: Benedictus *(Missa L'homme armé super voces musicales)*

In the following example from Morales the imitation is at the fifth and in stretto. The cambiata in measure 19 is made prominent by its immediate imitation in the second voice, followed by a second cambiata and imitation a step lower. Notice the lengthy imitation of each theme, the dovetailed cadences, the suspensions and other dissonances.

Example 7-21
Morales: Agnus Dei *(Missa Tristezas me matan)*

In addition to the preceding examples shown, the following duos from the *Penitential Psalms* should be sung and analyzed.

In the fifth verse of Psalm III (p. 90), the second voice enters in imitation at the fifth above. After the Phrygian cadence in measure 10, the imitation is at the unison, concluding with an extensive melisma on the words *insipientiae meae*, suggesting unbridled foolishness.

The setting of verse 9, Psalm IV (p. 144), contains an interesting chain suspension in the lower voice in measures 15–18, inverted in measures 19–21. On the word *humilitate*, the halting descent to low E is suggestive of deep humility.

8
Three-Voice Counterpoint

Harmonic Resources

The principles of intervallic relationships between two voices, as previously observed in two-voice counterpoint, continue with the addition of a third part. The analysis of the intervals is made from the lowest part to each of the upper parts, and the foundation of the writing continues to be consonance.

The addition of a third part creates a basis for chordal sound. The harmony of sixteenth-century music, however, is a result of melodic movement and does not, except at cadence points, follow a predictable pattern of root movement. Dissonance temporarily interrupts consonance and is introduced in the specific ways already discussed in two-voice writing. Interval analysis between the lowest part and each of the upper parts reveals that a triad may appear in first inversion with the root above the fifth in the upper voices, as shown in example 8-1. The interval between the bass and the tenor is a major or minor third, between the bass and the alto is a major or minor sixth. That there is a fourth between the two upper voices is accepted in the style, provided each voice is consonant with the bass. The upper parts may between them have the root and fifth of a diminished or an augmented triad, but the diminished or augmented interval must not be between the lowest voice and either of the upper parts.

All of the triads in the modes, untransposed as well as transposed, are available. Major and minor triads are used in root position and in first inversion. The second inversion, because of the dissonant fourth with the lowest part, is not available except with the fourth as a correctly treated dissonance. Diminished triads are less frequently employed than major and minor triads, while the augmented triad is used sparingly for dramatic or pictorial effects. Augmented and diminished triads are used in first inversion only.

Example 8-1

Although the triads are generally complete, at times a member is omitted and another member is doubled. In major and minor triads the doubled note is more often the root or the fifth, but melodic movement may cause a third to be doubled. A leading tone, whether natural as in the Lydian and Ionian modes, or created by *musica ficta* in the other modes, is not doubled. In augmented and diminished triads, the third is usually doubled. B♭ may be doubled. The B minor triad rarely appears because the tritone is corrected by lowering B, not by raising F.

Observe the intervallic relationships in example 8-2. The triads are generally complete; where there is a member omitted, the doubling varies, but notes with accidentals are not doubled. In measure 9, an augmented triad is used. It is complete, and in first inversion. Between the upper voices is a diminished fourth, but between the lowest voice and each of the two upper voices there is consonance. Sing the piece, observing the harmonic sound resulting from the individual voice movement.

Example 8-2

Victoria: *Eram quasi agnus innocens* (responsary)

Translation: All my enemies think evil against me: they speak evil words toward me, saying. . . .

In three-voice writing the spacing between voices is generally close, and the upper voices are rarely more than an octave apart. The voices sometimes cross and create an interesting coloristic effect in doing so, particularly when it is the lowest voice that moves above an adjacent voice. When crossing occurs, the intervals are judged from the lowest pitch sounding at the time, rather than from the voice that before the crossing had been the lowest part.

The chords were largely generated by melodic movement, frequently in stepwise root relationships. In later styles, root movement by second or third relationship occurs far less often than in the sixteenth century, accounting, in part, for the difference in harmonic sound.

The addition of a third part makes it possible to have an octave or unison between two of the voices on any beat, provided the doubled notes are approached and left by contrary or oblique motion. Parallel unisons, octaves, and fifths are forbidden in the style. Each melodic line is allowed to express its individuality through a preponderance of contrary and oblique motion. The independence of the lines is quickly lost in passages of similar motion; passages in which all voices skip in the same direction are avoided by having one voice move by step.

Cadence

The addition of a third part to the clausula vera type of phrase ending makes possible the cadence structure later referred to as the authentic cadence. An examination of example 8-3 will reveal variations in the cadence resulting from inversion, doubling, and voice leading. Notice the tripled final caused by combining the bass movement, 5–1, with the clausula vera in the upper voices. The leading-tone cadence occurs only when the lowest voice in a first inversion leading-tone chord descends by step to the final, and the leading tone in an upper voice ascends by half step to the final. The diminished fifth between the root and the fifth is in the upper voices. The presence of the leading tone in the lowest voice necessitates a dominant chord in first inversion. The last measure shows the upper voice in the penultimate chord moving to a third instead of to a doubled final. The leading tone is usually delayed by a suspension.

Example 8-3

While the authentic type of cadence requires a leading-tone movement into the final note, another cadence favored by sixteenth-century composers did not. This cadence, later called the plagal cadence, involves a penultimate triad whose root is a fifth below the final. When the penultimate chord is complete, the final chord is incomplete, and the reverse is true when the penultimate chord is incomplete. The final plagal cadence often occurs following an authentic cadence, suggesting the later Amen cadence attached to hymns or, when extended, the final coda in the subdominant as used in the classical period.

Example 8-4

Because of its half step above the final, the cadence on the final of the Phrygian mode, though a clausula vera type, sounds unlike the other cadences. The penultimate triad is minor, and the suspension that is usually present is delaying a root that is a whole step below the final. In the untransposed modes, the cadence occurs not only on E, but also on A when preceded by B♭. In the transposed Phrygian, the cadence is on A and also on D when preceded by E♭.

Example 8-5

When the penultimate chord of the authentic cadence changes direction, the root moving up or down by step instead of by leap to the final, the resulting cadence is referred to as a deceptive cadence. In later music a deceptive cadence consists of a dominant chord ascending to the submediant, but in the sixteenth century the dominant sometimes descended to the subdominant, as it sounds to present-day hearers. In example 8-6 may be seen the deceptive cadence in its ascending and descending forms.

Example 8-6

In all final cadences both the penultimate and the final chords are in root position, with the exception of the Phrygian, in which the penultimate chord is in first inversion. In the final chord, the third, if present, is major, musica ficta having been applied to the Dorian, Phrygian, and Aeolian thirds.

Interior cadences may be of the leading-tone type with first inversion penultimate chord, or other authentic types with either or both chords inverted. The deceptive cadence also belongs to the nonfinal type of phrase ending.

The continuous flow of the music is preserved by the overlapping of the phrase ending in one voice and the phrase beginning in another voice. When the leading tone is present, the voice carrying it continues to the cadence final. The other two voices at separate times are interrupted by rests. If the piece is imitative, each reentering voice imitates the new subject. Observe the overlapping in the interior cadence in example 8-7. In measure 11, the Phrygian cadence on D is completed; after a rest the lower voice reenters with a new theme on *tímentibus,* the others imitating at the fourth following a rest in each part.

Example 8-7
Victoria: *Magnificat primi toni*

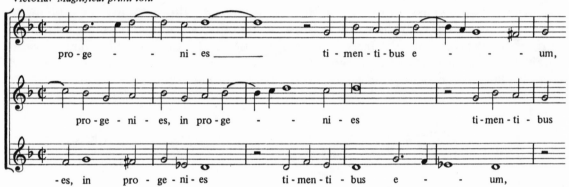

Another example of the interrupted cadence may be seen in the *Penitential Psalms,* III, verse 10, measures 9–12 (p. 100). The outer voices move to the doubled final while the middle voice rests and reenters with a new theme. After rests the outer voices imitate the new theme in widely spaced points of entry.

EXERCISE

The following cadences contain errors. Locate them, and suggest ways of correcting them.

Example 8-8

Dissonance

It is in the relationship of the lowest part to each of the upper parts that dissonance or consonance is analyzed. Consonant agreement between the parts is the usual sound, and it is against this concord that discord makes its impact. With the exception of the nota cambiata, all dissonances are approached and left by stepwise movement. The essential characteristics of each dissonance and its interactions with others are discussed in this section.

SUSPENSIONS

The cadence structures of the sixteenth century were generally strengthened and ornamented by the addition of suspensions. The suspensions already discussed in two-voice counterpoint, 7–6, 2–3, 4–3, are employed in three-voice counterpoint, as are also other suspensions not possible in two voices.

In example 8-9 intervals that may be present in addition to the 7–6 suspension, all analyzed from the bass, are shown. Observe the fifth in example 8-9C, which, though consonant with the bass, moves when the resolution note, the sixth, arrives. The move prevents dissonance with the resolution note. The other voice may have the third, the fifth, or the octave above the bass. The bass, as shown in example 8-9D, may move to another consonant note as the resolution note arrives. The 7–6 suspension is associated with the Phrygian cadence and also with the leading-tone cadence.

Example 8-9

The 2–3 suspension is the only suspension in the lowest voice. In addition to the necessary second or ninth, it may have a third, a fourth, a fifth, or a sixth. These intervals are all consonant with either the suspended note or the resolution note. The third and the sixth are dissonant with the resolution note and must move to another note on the resolution beat.

Example 8-10

Although the 4–3 suspension is not useful for final cadences in two-voice writing, it is of primary importance in writing for more than two voices. The authentic cadence, when the clausula vera is between the upper voices, contains a 4–3 suspension into the leading tone, which is the third of the penultimate chord. In addition to the suspended fourth, there may be a fifth, a sixth, or an octave above the bass. The sixth moves to the fifth in the resolution chord. Example 8-11 shows the 4–3 with variations in the third voice and the resolution chord. Notice the suspended tritone in example 8-11D and the change of bass in example 8-11E.

Example 8-11

In the 9–8 and 2–1 suspensions the resolution note doubles the pitch of the lowest voice already present on the suspension beat; this differs from other suspensions in each of which the resolution note is generally not present while the suspension is sounding. The 9–8 and 2–1 suspensions are used infrequently in three voices. The intervals in addition to the ninth or second are generally a third or a sixth above the lowest voice (example 8-12A).

Suspensions may be combined, provided the suspended voices do not move in parallel fifths. In combining the 7–6 and the 4–3, fifths occur if the 4–3 is above the 7–6, but can be avoided by the use of a portamento resolution of either of the suspensions. The combination of the 9–8 and the 4–3 is more often used; however, double suspensions in three voices are less frequent than in four or more voices (example 8-12B, C, D).

Example 8-12

EXERCISE

Using the following melody alternately as the upper, middle, or lower part, add the two other parts, constructing suspensions at the points indicated by "S." A suspension may be in a voice other than the given voice, and additional dissonance should be included where appropriate.

Example 8-13

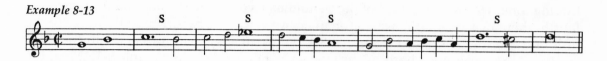

Two other dissonant structures with suspension characteristics are available in three voices: the $^6_5$ chord and the so-called consonant fourth.

The fourth, though normally considered a dissonance, may become the preparation of a 4–3 suspension in the circumstances permitted in the structure of the consonant fourth. The device consists of a fourth approached stepwise on the weak beat over a sustained bass tone. It is tied into the following strong beat, where with the addition of a fifth in the other voice, it becomes a 4–3 suspension. The sustaining bass part must be sounding at least one beat prior to the introduction of the fourth and must be continued at least four beats while the preparation, suspension, and resolution are completed. In example 8-14 the normal form of the device is shown. Notice the doubling of the fourth by a half-note passing tone in the first measure and by a lower auxiliary tone in the second measure.

Example 8-14

EXERCISE

Complete the measures in example 8-15, employing a consonant fourth over each note that sustains four beats.

Example 8-15

The presence of a sixth and a fifth in the upper voices, each consonant with the lowest voice but dissonant with each other, is the basis of the $^6_5$ structure. Because of the dissonance of a second or a seventh between the upper parts, one of them, usually the fifth, is treated as a suspension. The $^6_5$ occurs on beat one or three, with the fifth prepared on beat two or four. As the suspended fifth resolves, the bass moves up a step, creating with the resolution note a third. If the sixth is stationary, a root-position triad results (example 8-16A). If the sixth rises a second as the bass rises, the chord of resolution is a first-inversion triad (example 8-16B). The lowest voice may leap down a third under the resolution (example 8-16C), or down a fifth (example 8-16D); the resolution triad may be diminished (example 8-16E); the suspended fifth may be diminished (example 8-16F).

Example 8-16

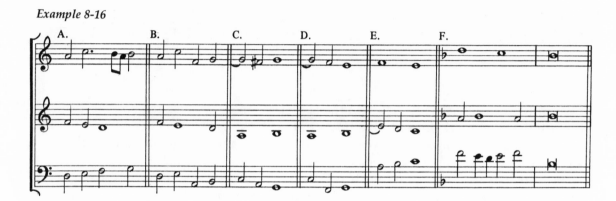

EXERCISE

Complete the counterpoint in example 8-17, employing a $^6_5$ suspension with the fifth prepared as indicated by the figured bass.

Example 8-17

A $^6_5$ suspension may be followed by a consonant fourth with the same bass note serving for both suspensions. This sequence of suspensions is possible when the fifth resolves but the bass does not ascend under the resolution note. The resolution of the fifth to a fourth over the sustaining bass creates the preparation note of the consonant-fourth structure.

Example 8-18
Victoria: Benedictus *(Missa Ave maris stella)*

An infrequent device is the ⁶₅ with the sixth prepared. Because the sixth resolves to the fifth that is already present, this treatment of the ⁶₅ is less effective than when the fifth is the prepared note. It is frequently followed by another suspension on the next strong beat, as in example 8-19, measure 11.

The *Esurientes* section from a Palestrina Magnificat provides an opportunity to observe a number of dissonances. In measure 11, a ⁶₅ suspension with the sixth prepared is followed by a ⁶₅ with the fifth prepared. A ninth suspended in measure 22 is followed in measure 23 by an augmented triad on beat one, a consonant-fourth preparation on beat two, with additional dissonance created by a fifth entering on beat two. Consecutive seconds, with a lower auxiliary tone between them, are in the upper voices. Singing the example after analysis will increase the awareness and understanding of the dissonance.

Translation: He has filled the hungry with good things: and the rich he has sent away empty.

Example 8-19
Palestrina: Esurientes implevit bonis *(Magnificat primi toni)*

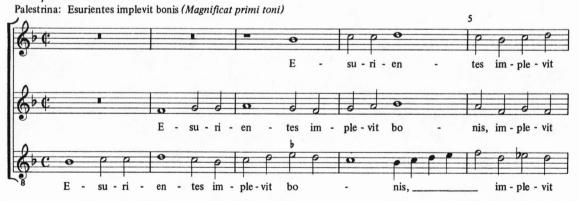

PASSING TONES

As previously discussed in two-voice counterpoint, the half-note passing tone occurs ascending or descending on beat two or four in relation to a sustaining note double its length. The passing tone, if moving in similar note-value with a harmony note that leaps, must be consonant with the note that leaps (example 8-20A).

Double half-note passing tones may occur in similar motion, thirds or sixths apart, or in contrary motion, in unisons, thirds, sixths, or octaves (example 8-20B).

Example 8-20

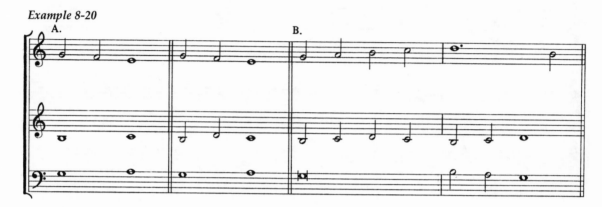

Quarter notes in two voices that move simultaneously are generally consonant with each other but may be dissonant with the other voice as accented passing tones, descending on beat two or four, or unaccented passing tones on the second half of any beat, ascending or descending (example 8-21A).

A stepwise quarter-note passage in one voice may contain passing tones dissonant with the bass and also with the other voice. If the other voice leaps, it must be consonant with the bass but may be dissonant with the quarter notes. If there is a leap within the quarter-note passage, the note approached or left by leap, with the exception of the cambiata, must be consonant with both voices (example 8-21B).

A passage of four or more quarter notes, one of which is an accented passing tone, must change direction by step following the resolution of the passing tone. The quarter-note passage may be moving in unequal values with another part, creating consecutive dissonance with both parts (example 8-21C).

Quarter-note passing tones occur in any voice. An upper voice may have the sustaining notes against which the lowest voice has passing-tone dissonance (example 8-21D).

Example 8-21

AUXILIARY (NEIGHBOR) NOTES

As discussed in two-voice writing, the auxiliary tone occurs on the second half of any beat, ascending or descending. In addition to its dissonance with the lowest voice, it may be dissonant with an offbeat note in another voice. In example 8-22A an auxiliary is dissonant with a portamento following a suspension. Other instances of auxiliary tones interacting with offbeat movement in either of the other voices may be seen in example 8-22B.

Example 8-22

CAMBIATAS

The cambiata, its dissonant second note left by leap, may begin on any beat; therefore, the dissonance may coincide with the *portamento* on the second half of beat one or three, or with the other offbeat dissonances. Example 8-23A shows a *cambiata* on the half beat of three sounding with an unaccented passing tone. In example 8-23B a *cambiata* coincides with a *portamento*. The note left by leap is generally consonant with similar-moving note-values in another part, although both may be dissonant with the bass or a sustaining upper part.

Example 8-23

PORTAMENTOS

Usually employed as an ornament forecasting the resolution of a suspension, the *portamento* is more often a consonance. It may be employed in two voices where double suspensions occur. When used as a melodic idiom without the presence of a suspension, the *portamento* is derived from consonance on the first half of beats one or three and may be either consonant or dissonant. A *portamento* is likely to be consonant with another similar-moving note-value. Notice in foregoing example 8-23B, measure 3, double *portamentos* moving in thirds, one ornamenting a suspension resolution and consonant with the bass, the other dissonant with the bass, but the two in consonant agreement. In the same measure a *portamento* is combined with a passing tone.

EIGHTH NOTES

Occurring only on the second half of a beat, approached and left by step, eighth-note pairs frequently coincide with offbeat dissonance in other voices. Although either eighth note may be dissonant, the second of the two as a passing tone or neighboring tone is more often dissonant with a quarter note in another part (example 8-24A). Simultaneous pairs may occur, usually moving in thirds or sixths (example 8-24B). With the addition of *musica ficta,* the first of a pair of eighth notes embellishing a suspension resolution may be an augmented or diminished interval in relation to another part (example 8-24C).

Example 8-24

Imitation

The pitch relations and the time intervals between imitating voices as observed in two-voice counterpoint continue in three-voice counterpoint. The imitations occur at various intervals, but more often in fourth or fifth relationships, reflecting the vocal ranges of adjacent parts. Points of entry are frequently the final and the dominant notes of the mode. Voices enter at irregular time intervals from each other. The third entry is likely to be farther from the second entry than the second entry is from the first. Notice in example 8-25 that the second voice enters in stretto, while the third voice enters two

Example 8-25
Lasso: *Penitential Psalms,* I, verse 3

measures later. The mode is Dorian, and the imitation is D–A–A, the latter two notes suggesting soprano and tenor whose ranges are an octave apart. In examples 8-25 and 8-26 ¢ is rendered in relation to the whole note.

In example 8-26 the imitation is mirrored. The imitating voices enter on A, the third voice shortening the initial note. The subject is Hypophrygian melody, and A is its dominant.

Example 8-26
Lasso: *Penitential Psalms*, IV, verse 12

Divisions of the text create phrase groups of irregular length. Internal cadences are generally of the interrupted type, with the next phrase introduced in one voice while the others sustain the essential cadence notes. New interior themes frequently begin on weak beats and may begin with a passage of quarter notes. The cadence points common to the mode are used, as well as a variety of cadence formulas.

Examine the opening imitations in the setting of the *Benedictus* that follows. The opening pitches of the three entering voices, D–A–A, suggest the usual distance between ranges of adjacent voices, and also state the Dorian final and dominant. Notice the tonal adjustment in the lower voice in measure 4, and in the upper part in measure 5. The original fifth, D–A, is imitated by a fourth, A–D. In measure 8 the upper part rests without cadencing and reenters on the weak beat to repeat the phrase of text with a new motive. The upper part had been the last to state the opening theme but is the first voice to introduce the phrase repetition. The other voices enter in stretto, again using D–A imitating A–D. The time value of the first note is halved in the imitating voices, causing the melisma to begin on a weak beat instead of the strong beat as in the original statement of the motive. An imperfect cadence is reached in measure 14 with a clausula vera in the upper voices on A. While the highest voice holds A, the middle voice rests, reentering with a new theme and the next phrase of text. The truncated cadence enables the new theme to be presented and imitated without an interruption of the flow of music.

Example 8-27
Victoria: Benedictus *(Missa Surge propera)*

Translation: Blessed is He who comes.

In example 8-28, the second and third entries are equal in time-distance from each other. The second voice imitates the subject at the unison, and the third voice imitates at the fifth. After the cadence in measure 9, the lower voice rests and reenters with a new theme, which is imitated, with modifications, by the other voices. The concluding cadence, the clausula vera in the upper voices, moves to a tripled final. Notice the textual repetition in the upper voices, while the lowest voice, which entered last, completes the text before arriving at the cadence in measure 9. The lower voices repeat the last phrase to balance the measure of rest in the upper voice before its entry with the second theme.

Example 8-28
Palestrina: *Me menavit* (Lamentation)

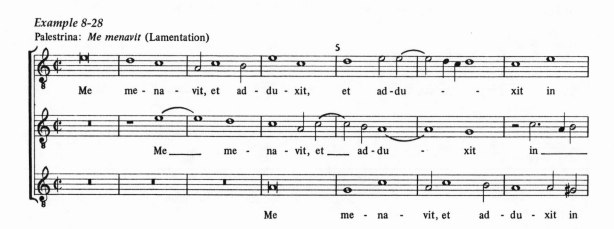

Translation: He has led me and brought me into darkness, not into light.

EXERCISE

Compose for three adjacent voices a setting of either of the text fragments given below. There should be an imitative opening, an interior cadence with overlapping entry of the second subject and points of imitation, and a continuation in free counterpoint to the final cadence. Study the preceding examples in their use of text and contrapuntal resources. Eight to twelve measures should be an appropriate length.

Text: (1) Et a-ni-ma me-a tur-ba-ta est val-de.
     (And my soul is troubled exceedingly)
The text may be in two sections, the division after *mea*.

     (2) Holy is his name, Amen.

Three-Voice Compositions

Complete three-voice movements are included in the following pages, providing illustrations of a variety of contrapuntal treatments. In addition to these, reference is made to designated verse settings in the *Penitential Psalms* with suggestions of passages for analysis.

The metrical organization discussed up to this point has been structured largely around the breve and its division into four half-note beats, with the suspension dissonance assigned to beats one and three, the passing tone to two and four, and the other dissonances to the offbeats. As stated at the beginning of this study, the style is presented initially in historical white mensural notation in order that the manner in which it was originally written and may still be seen in existing primary sources may be understood. But it has not been the intention of this study to perpetuate the use of white notation as the only means of representing sixteenth-century music. The elements of the style as studied to this point may be understood more fully if perceived in still another meter, and it is strongly recommended that the opportunities provided in the succeeding pages for singing, hearing, and analyzing the style in both 4/2 and 4/4 meters be fully utilized. The viewpoint underlying this approach, as stated previously, is that the meter merely defines the mathematical duration of notes in relation to each other, but the rhythm is the plan of organization of procedures regarding melodic movement, harmony, dissonance and cadence according to the requirements of the style. The requirements are not tied to any one metrical representation.

Before singing the following pieces in 4/4 meter, observe that the eighth note here replaces the quarter note as the half beat and when on the second half of the beat is not approached by ascending leap. The offbeat pair now consists of two sixteenth notes to be treated stepwise. It should be noted here that secular music in the latter part of the sixteenth century was at times written with the quarter note as the unit of beat. Palestrina's second book of madrigals, published in 1586, was so notated.

The first composition is a section from a Mass by Morales. The upper voice initiates the theme, which is then imitated a fifth below by the lower voice. The middle voice enters after a longer time-distance, imitating the preceding voice at the unison. When the word *descendit* appears, the melody plunges downward, and the imitation, with overlapping phrases repeating the word, makes the descent from heaven inescapably pictorial. The concluding cadence further reinforces the descent with the movement to the final low note of the upper voice.

Example 8-29

Morales: Credo *(Missa Desilde al cavallero)*

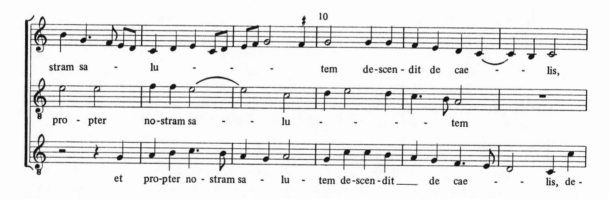

Translation: Who for us men and for our salvation came down from heaven.

The following three-voice motets in the *Penitential Psalms* are suggested for analysis and singing:

Psalm I, verse 3 (pp. 21–22). Notice the cambiata in measure 19. The final phrase of text, *sed tu Domine usque quo?* (but thou, O Lord, how long?) takes a surprising turn to cadence on the dominant, its inconclusiveness coinciding with the question. (Translation: And my soul is troubled exceedingly; but thou, O Lord, how long?)

Psalm II, verse 6 (pp. 54–55), in Mode 2, transposed. Voices entering in stretto present the word *Dixi* (I said) followed by rests as in speech rhythm. The pronouncement that follows begins homorhythmically and then expands melodically on syllables of *meam Domino* (my God). In measures 22–29, on *peccati mei* (my sin), each voice has a long melisma, implying extensive sin, concluding with a unified repeating of the words and a plagal cadence on G with minor penultimate chord. (Translation: I said I will confess against myself my injustice to the Lord: and thou has forgiven the wickedness of my sin.)

Psalm V, verse 14 (pp. 188–189). Beginning with points of imitation in which the subject is mirrored, the syllable *sur* in the words *tu exsurgens* (thou shall arise) is extended in wide-ranged melisma. The first cadence overlaps with a new subject in the alto, which is imitated at the interval of a seventh by the tenor and at the sixth by the bass and continues in modified imitation until the conclusion. (Translation: Thou shalt arise and have mercy on Sion, for it is time to have mercy on it, for the time is come.)

Psalm VI, verse 7 (p. 230). The composer's mastery of the design of his setting of the psalms as well as of contrapuntal skills is nowhere more apparent than in Psalm VI. He placed the psalm in the sixth mode and used the sixth psalm-tone as cantus firmus. In the seventh verse, the psalm-tone is in the upper voice, the lower voices imitating each other in stretto. The continuously sustaining upper voice is offset by the melismatic passages in the lower voices. The final plagal cadence contains a doubled final and a fifth. (Translation: Because with the Lord there is mercy: and with him plentiful redemption.)

Psalm VII, verse 3 (p. 240). The motet begins with a stepwise ascent of an octave in the outer voices, the upper voice moving a beat ahead of the lower voice, creating a passage of seven first-inversion triads. There are double suspensions in measure 6, a consonant fourth in measures 7–8. At the cadence is a suspension structure suggestive of the cadential second-inversion-to-dominant formula of later times. (Translation: For the enemy hath persecuted my soul: he hath brought down my life to earth.)

Psalm VIII, motet 3 (pp. 281–284). This psalm has a different construction from the first seven. Its principal relation to the others is that it completes the modal cycle of eight psalms in eight modes. Lasso uses the complete texts of Psalms 148 and 150 for only four motets, thereby making each a considerably longer piece. The second motet combines the last four verses of Psalm 148 with the first verse of Psalm 150. It begins with the voices in collective rhythm as the young men and maidens (*juvenes et virgines*) are addressed. On the words *filiis Israel populo appropinquanti sibi* (to the children of Israel, a people approaching to him) the rhythm becomes jerky, with offbeat syncopation. At the words *laudate Dominum* (praise ye the Lord) the rhythmic agitation subsides, points of imitation introduce a smoothly flowing melody, and the voices continue in free imitation to a final plagal cadence.

(Translation: Young men and maidens: let the old with the younger praise the name of the Lord: for his name alone is exalted. The praise of him is above heaven and earth: and he hath exalted the horn to his people. A hymn to all his saints: to the children of Israel, a people approaching to him. Praise ye the Lord in his holy places, praise ye him in the firmament of his power.)

The *Benedictus* of Palestrina in example 8-30 contains a canon at the octave between the outer voices. The sign 𝄋 indicates the point at which the canonic imitation begins and is used again to indicate the point at which it ends. Notice the $\begin{smallmatrix}6\\3\end{smallmatrix}$ chord in measure 19. In measure 28 the consonant fourth over the dominant is followed by a plagal cadence, its minor penultimate chord on G. The Mass is in the transposed Dorian mode.

Example 8-30
Palestrina: Benedictus *(Missa O Rex gloriae)*

Translation: Blessed is He who comes in the name of the Lord.

The opening imitation of the *Et misericordia* setting by Victoria is symmetrical in the time-spacing of the opening voice entries. The beginning notes, E–F–D–E, in the middle voice, imitated on A–B♭–G–A, create a Phrygian awareness, and quietly suggest the reverence expressed in the words. Subsequent themes are overlapping in their entries, and cadences are reached on A, C, D, and F, concluding with a plagal cadence on A. Notice the voice crossing in measures 29 and 30, where the lower voice moves above the sustaining middle voice to form a $\frac{6}{5}$-consonant-fourth sequence. The beautiful effect is underscored by the scalewise ascent of a ninth in the lower voice to the preparation note of the $\frac{6}{5}$.

Example 8-31
Victoria: Et misericordia *(Magnificat tertii toni)*

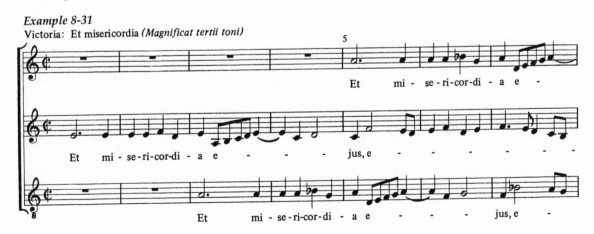

Translation: And his mercy is on them that fear him, throughout all generations.

The example from William Byrd provides another opportunity to experience meter as a tool for notating rhythm, rather than as an arbiter of a style. A singing of the Benedictus will reveal that the text is clearly presented and that there is an interesting rhythmic vitality. A difference can be felt, however, between this piece and examples from Palestrina. In the leaps into the subdivisions of the beat, it is apparent that Byrd is not following the melodic strictures of the style as closely as Palestrina. Notice the cross relation in measures 6–7.

Example 8-32
Byrd: Benedictus *(Mass for three voices)*

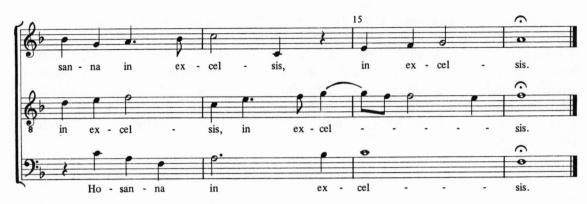

san - na in ex - cel - sis, in ex - cel - sis.

in ex - cel - sis, in ex - cel - - - - sis.

Ho - san - na in ex - cel - - - sis.

Translation: Blessed is He who comes in the name of the Lord.

EXERCISES

1. In the following composition find the errors in melodic line, intervallic relations, text setting, and procedures relating to dissonance.

Example 8-33

Ho - san - - - na, — Ho - san - na _____

Ho - san - - na, Ho - san - - na _____

Ho - san - na, Ho - san - na _____

2. Write opening points of imitation for three voices on the subjects below, taken from works of Palestrina. Different features of imitation should be used as, for example: No. 1 in free imitation; No. 2 in mirror; No. 3, in free imitation in stretto; No. 4, in free imitation at the unison. Continue each in free counterpoint to a cadence. Notice the translation of ¢ in the first three melodies to note values in relation to the whole note.

Example 8-34

A.

B.

C.

D.

3. Reproduced in example 8-35 is a section from a Gloria of Lasso. The subject entries and reentries are included. Complete the counterpoint, continuing the imitation as long as possible before going into nonimitative counterpoint.

Example 8-35

4. Following the contrapuntal resources studied and the sound of the style experienced through singing, write a complete three-voice composition. Use the Latin text of any of the compositions recently sung, observing the division into smaller units for repetition, for interior cadences, and for imitative reentry. Follow the syllabification as used in the printed texts. Recite the words, feeling the syllables of stress and appropriateness for sustaining. The composition should be imitative, both initially and in the reentry of voices after interior cadences, and should include the devices of dissonance as previously discussed. If preferable, an English text may be chosen, using the same procedures as described above. Write in either 4/2 or 4/4 meter.

9
Counterpoint in Four Voices: The Motet

Familiar Style

Passages in which the voices move uniformly in regard to note values and syllables of text are found in the longer sections of the Mass. Other compositions, such as hymns, motets, and responses, may be wholly or in part written in a syllabic, chordal manner. Such writing is designated variously as familiar style *(stile familiare)*, homorhythmic, and homophonic.

There are advantages to text setting in familiar style, in that the words may be heard more clearly, more words may be set in a short time-span, and the unified sound creates a sense of dignity, or worship, or other single effect. However, individual voice movement at times asserts itself through dissonance, or reiteration of syllable, or agogic accent.

Aspects of Four-Voice Texture

The addition of a fourth voice brings about the necessity for doubling a triadic member. Although in familiar style the root is more often doubled in root-position triads, there seems to be no general procedure for selecting the member to be doubled other than melodic movement and avoidance of doubling a leading tone. Although there is generally close spacing between the upper voices, the melodic character of each voice is expressed freely with occasional wide spacing and crossing of voices. Parallel perfect fifths and octaves are not used.

The root movement is nonfunctional in the sense of the common-practice hierarchy of chords. There is no tonal center toward which chords must move, except as cadences offer points of repose. At times, however, in passages of root movements by fourths and fifths, the security of later harmonic organization is felt. The structure of cadences is predictable and adds stability to successions of sounds that may seem without focus. Unlike later music, there is frequent root movement by seconds and thirds. Authentic cadences more often contain the 4–3 suspension, and the fourth voice is likely to be a doubling of the bassus, with the clausula vera in the upper parts. In suspension and cadence formulas, neither the suspended note nor the leading tone is doubled. Example

9–1 illustrates suspension and cadence approach typical of four-voice writing. Examine the doublings, the manner in which the doubled notes are approached and left, the dissonance, and the close spacing in the upper parts. This passage is taken from a madrigal of Palestrina, which, although secular, contains the same compositional techniques as are used with sacred texts. The original meter signature was **C**, with the quarter note as the unit of beat.

Example 9-1
Palestrina: *Se non fusse il pensier* (madrigal)

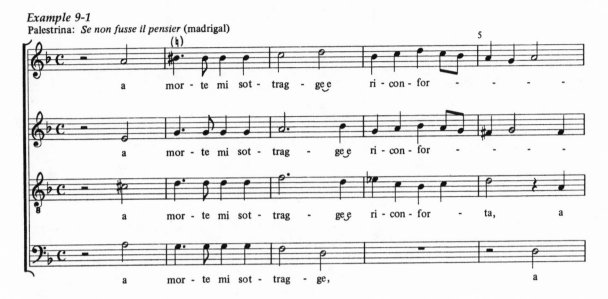

The following four-voice passage illustrates the movement of the voices chordally with one voice at times differing rhythmically from the others. Notice the use of C♯ in the first chord. Musica ficta in four-voice writing may be coloristic rather than restricted to the cadential leading tone. The descending stepwise root movement found in measures 1–2 and 4 is not unusual in Renaissance writing. The motet is in the Dorian mode. A Dorian melodic idiom, descending consecutive leaps of a perfect fifth and a minor third, may be seen in the second-tenor part, measures 4–5.

Example 9-2
Lasso: *Penitential Psalms,* I, Verse 10

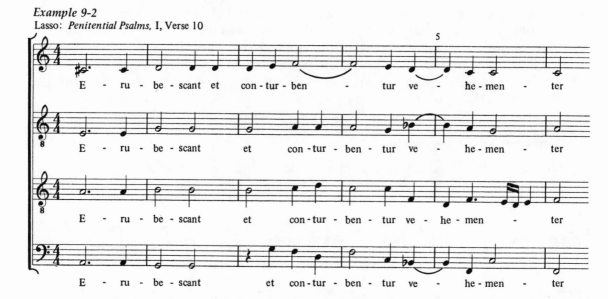

In the *Penitential Psalms* the following four-voice motets in familiar style are suggested, with brief commentary, for further study.

Psalm I, verse 4 (p. 22), has a number of root movements by descending second. The consonant fourth over the dominant bass, measures 17–18, is left by descending step. The suspension in the final cadence is in augmentation, followed by a final chord without a third. (Translation: And my soul is troubled exceedingly; but thou, O Lord, how long?)

Psalm II, verse 4 (p. 49), begins in familiar style. In measure 17 points of imitation initiate a somewhat agitated theme on the words *dum configitur spina* (while the thorn is fastened). It is used motivically by all voices for the next thirteen measures. In each of the root-position chords the root is doubled. (Translation: For day and night thy hand was heavy upon me: I am turned in my anguish, whilst the thorn is fastened.)

Psalm V, verse 4 (p. 173). The chordal setting of the first phrase is abruptly ended on an offbeat, followed by rests in all voices. A description of *Quia defecerunt sicut fuma* (for my days are vanished like smoke) is implied. The final cadence is a bit surprising when the dominant note in the bass descends a second, after which a plagal, not the expected authentic cadence is achieved. (Translation: For my days are vanished like smoke: and my bones are grown dry like fuel for the fire.)

EXERCISE

Write a four-voice setting in familiar style of each of the following texts as specified. Use either 4/2 or 4/4 meter.

1. For everything there is a season, and a time for everything under the sun. (Aeolian mode, Phrygian cadence on A.)

2. Happy is the man that findeth wisdom. (Lydian mode, perfect authentic cadence.)

3. Understanding is a wellspring of life unto him that hath it. (Dorian mode, leading tone cadence.)

Imitation

In four-voice imitation, the points of entry continue to be largely in fourth and fifth relationships. Imitation may be found at other intervals, however, with the unison and the octave perhaps next in frequency. Time-distance between entries varies; it is sometimes symmetrical, sometimes asymmetrical, and the distance between points of entry initially may not be retained for succeeding subjects and imitations. Frequently the voices are paired, the second entering soon after the beginning of the first in the usual fourth or fifth relationship. Sometimes they are canonic, or at least continue in exact imitation for some distance until the third voice enters. The third and fourth voices have the same relationship to each other as had the previous pair. As they present the theme and imitation, voices one and two may drop out and reenter with a new theme. The entry of the second pair of voices is likely to vary the rhythmic design, as when a theme on beat one is imitated on beat three. Example 9-3 from Palestrina illustrates the device of paired voice entries.

Example 9-3
Palestrina: Quia respexit *(Magnificat octavi toni)*

Two themes are sometimes used for the opening imitation. They may enter simultaneously, or in close succession, continuing in free counterpoint for several measures before the third and fourth voices enter imitating them. In example 9-4 the opening subjects, a fifth apart, present the two themes in a long enough time-span to allow them to be recognized when voices three and four imitate them.

Example 9-4
Palestrina: Et exultavit *(Magnificat secundi toni)*

The opening point of imitation in the *Deo Gratias* of William Byrd presents a pairing of the two inner voices imitating in stretto. The outer voices in quick succession introduce a second theme after which they, too, imitate the first theme and the first two voices take the second theme. The contrasting nature of the two themes makes the design immediately apparent when sung.

Example 9-5
Byrd: *Deo Gratias*

Translation: Thanks be to God.

See also, in the *Penitential Psalms*, Psalm III, verse 20 (pp. 119–120). Opening points of mirrored imitation at the fifth are followed by chordal movement. The words *et multi-plicati sunt* (and are multiplied) are set in a repetitious reciting manner, then repeated rhythmically a step higher. (Translation: But my enemies live, and are stronger than I: but they that hate me wrongfully are multiplied.)

EXERCISES

1. Write, without text, the initial imitative section of a four-voice composition ending in a cadence appropriate to the mode. The imitation should continue in each voice until the next voice enters.

2. Using the two-phrase text supplied below, write an imitative composition with a cadence concluding the first phrase. The theme of the second phrase overlaps with the end of the first phrase, possibly taking part in the cadence, and continuing beyond, imitated by each voice until the next voice enters. Conclude with a cadence appropriate to the mode. The devices of dissonance should be included, and the meter may be 4/2 or 4/4.

Text: Ju-bi-la-te De-o, u-ni-ver-sa ter-ra.
(Be joyful in the Lord, O all the earth.)

Triple Meter

The meter of the preceding discussions has been entirely of one type, that of the division of the breve by two (*tempus imperfectum*) and the division of the semibreve by two (*prolatio imperfecta*), represented by the sign ₵. The absence of tempo markings and the uniformity of the notation could create in the present-day reader an impression of sameness, but a study of the proportional system reveals a precise means of varying the rhythmic scheme. It is likely that the beat varied little, but by an intricate system of proportions note values could be organized differently in relation to the beat. The use in present-day notation of ₵, *alla breve*, is a vestige of the proportional system. Its original meaning of making the breve, rather than the semibreve, the unit of time, is today interpreted as making the half note rather than the quarter note the unit of time.

The most generally used metrical signature was ₵, which divided the breve into two whole-note beats. The time signature did not indicate accentuation but instead indicated relationships with the breve. Therefore, the introduction of another metrical signature into a composition already organized around ₵ meant that relationships had changed, but the breve and the beat had not changed. When the meter signature Φ is employed in a composition already in ₵ meter, the breve continues to have two beats, but each beat now consists of three whole notes. The meter is generally indicated as 3/1, and the whole note is three times faster than in ₵. The signature O is generally interpreted as 3/2, and three half notes are equivalent to the whole note in ₵, making the half note one and one-half times faster than in ₵.

Divisions and subdivisions by three were considered perfect. *Modus*, or mood, referring to the relationship of the longa to the breve; *tempus*, or time, the breve to the whole note; and *prolatio*, or prolation, the whole note to the half note, would all be considered perfect if the long note in each instance was equal to three of the next smaller value.

Movements of the Mass, as well as motets and other compositions in duple time are sometimes interrupted by short sections in triple time. An examination of the placement of dissonance will reveal that the suspension occurs on any beat, but at the cadence it is likely to fall on the second beat. The speed is such that there is little offbeat activity. It would consist of passing tones, auxiliary notes, suspension ornamentations, and the second and fourth notes of the cambiata. Accented passing tones and the consonant fourth are not used. A section in triple time in which there is considerable offbeat activity would of necessity require a slower tempo.

Examples of proportional relations follow, with two measures of triple time equaling the preceding measure of duple time in each excerpt. In example 9-6 the 3:2 proportion becomes evident when the meter changes in the middle of a measure and three half notes replace the second whole note of the measure. The suspension on beat two with resolution on beat three is a typical cadence approach in triple time.

Example 9-6
Victoria: *O Regem coeli* (motet)

In Example 9-7 the original time values have been halved; the three half notes of a measure of 3/2 are equivalent to one half note of a measure of the preceding duple meter. A triple section is frequently in homorhythmic style, as in this passage from Anerio's motet. Felice Anerio sang at St. Peter's under Palestrina and in 1594 succeeded him as composer to the papal chapel.

Example 9-7
F. Anerio: *Alma Redemptoris Mater* (motet)

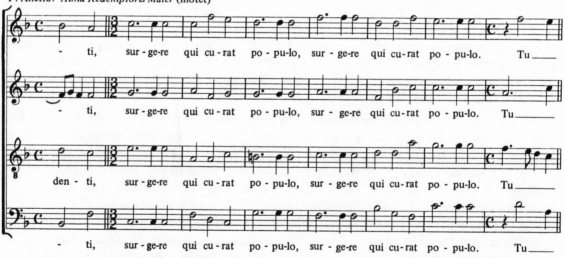

Additional examples of proportional relations may be found in the *Penitential Psalms*, I, verse 7 (p. 31); II, verse 14 (p. 72).

In addition to passages of triple meter inserted in a duple context and therefore governed by the proportional system, there are compositions or individual movements composed entirely in triple meter. When all note values are used the tempo must be modified to allow for articulation of the shorter notes, but when there is little subdivision of the beat, the tempo may be brisk as in the fast triple time.

In 3/1, when all note values are used, the rhythm is organized as in 2/1 (4/2) with another whole note added to the metric grouping. 3/1 is then treated as 6/2 (2 + 2 + 2). Considering the six half notes for placement of dissonance, the suspensions would be placed on beats one, three, and five, with the resolutions on two, four, and six. Other dissonance would be treated as in 4/2, with the third major beat carrying the same dissonance as the first two. It should be reiterated that here, as in 4/2, the beat is the whole note, but for ease in analysis and placement of dissonance the half notes are referred to as "beats," designating them strong and weak to differentiate between the first half of the whole-note beat and the second half.

Compositions in 3/2 have the half note as the unit of beat; however, the division of the whole note into three parts (perfect prolation) is the source of the three half notes. The breve has been divided into two groups (measures) of 3/2 each. For practical purposes the half note becomes the unit of beat. The suspensions occur on any beat, but at cadences they are usually on beat two.

The *Hosanna* that follows contains a striking use of *hemiola* (time values that are in relationship 3:2), a feature best analyzed aurally. There is a double canon between the soprano-alto and tenor-bass. The entire Mass from which the *Hosanna* is taken is canonic. A number of dissonances are employed in the texture and should be analyzed.

Example 9-8
Palestrina: Hosanna *(Missa ad fugam)*

The Motet

The sixteenth-century motet was a choral composition with sacred Latin text. The term *motet* dates from the twelfth and thirteenth centuries, when it was used to designate one of the contrapuntal voices added to the cantus firmus. Later it referred to a composition in which a voice sang a sacred text while another sang a secular text. By the sixteenth century the motet had become established as a choral composition with a Latin text, exclusive of the five sections of the Ordinary of the Mass. In practice, the text was divided into sections that were treated somewhat independently, were generally imitative, and frequently contained homorhythmic passages. The dovetailed cadences and reentry of voices connected the episodes, but at times the composer brought a section to a conclusion in all voices simultaneously, afterwards initiating a new and contrasting section. Thematic material is usually not returned. The interior cadences are brief, and the final cadence is generally made more conclusive by the employment of longer notes, root-position chords and ornamented suspensions, sometimes in augmentation.

Thematic materials of the motet frequently derive from plainsong. The technique of paraphrase in the early Renaissance involved the placing of a plainsong in its entirety in one voice. Later in the sixteenth century, the plainsong or portions of it are found in all the voices, producing points of imitation.

The study of the motet should be further enriched by the singing of complete representative examples. In the pages that follow, reference and analytical observations are offered on a motet from the *Penitential Psalms*, and two motets of Palestrina are provided with suggestions for analysis.

In Psalm I, verse 9 (p. 34) of the *Penitential Psalms*, Lasso places the upper voices in close relation to each other. Although employing only twenty measures, he expresses the assurance of answered prayer found in the text. In the Dorian mode, the beginning chord on D is major and moves to a G-major chord, followed by a descending stepwise progression to F. The half cadence on an E-major chord concludes the homorhythmic opening section and overlaps with the introduction in the alto of a brief repeated-note theme on *deprecationem* (supplication) imitated by the other voices and concluding with a cadence on A. The voices then move homorhythmically through a variety of chords, with the lowest voice having a repeated ascending-fifth leap on *orationem* (prayer). The phrase of text is repeated, and the other voices move differently, but the lowest again has the repeated leaps, this time leaping a fourth instead of a fifth. The final cadence on D is of the leading-tone type. Suspensions and passing-tone dissonances are used. In singing the motet the richness of the harmonic relations and the closely spaced voices should be noted. The text is so set that a specific mood of reflective prayerfulness is created. (Translation: The Lord hath heard my supplication: the Lord hath received my prayer.)

The motet, *Super flumina Babylonis*, a setting of Psalm 136 by Palestrina, expresses the sadness of the Hebrew people in exile. The psalm text was also used by Gombert and by William Byrd, who set verses 4 to 7 in answer to the setting of verses 1 to 3 sent to him by Philippe de Monte. Victoria also wrote a setting of the psalm for double choir and organ.

The text of *Super flumina Babylonis* is divided into five phrases, with points of imitation repeated, resulting in a series of double expositions. The textual division and form are as follows:

A .	Super flumina Babylonis	(mm. 1–14)
B .	illicsedimus, et flevimus	(mm. 14–18)
B′ .		(mm. 18–23)
C .	dem recordaremur tui Sion:	(mm. 23–29)
C′ .		(mm. 29–34)
C″ .		(mm. 34–39)
D .	in salicibus in midio ejus	(mm. 39–49)
D′ .		(mm. 49–55
E .	suspendimus organa nostra	(mm. 55–63)
E′ .		(mm. 63–71)

(Translation: (A) By the waters of Babylon (B) we sat down, and wept (C) when we remembered thee, O Sion: (D) there on the willow trees (E) we hung our harps.)

The motet *Lauda Sion* is a setting of Thomas Aquinas's sequence for the feast of Corpus Christi. The complete sequence has twenty-four versicles, and in the motet Palestrina uses only three of them, numbers 1, 2, and 23. The sequence melody is followed closely, although its beginning pitches, E–G, are changed in the motet to D–G. Palestrina uses the three musical units of versicle 1 as successive points of imitation, repeating them for versicle 2, except when the two lower voices in the latter part present the melodies from the first part in a modified double counterpoint. In the final versicle, consisting of five musical units, the first four are in familiar style and in triple time, the fifth contrapuntal in duple time and concluding with the Gregorian Amen.

Translation:

1. Sion, praise the Saviour,
   Praise the King and Shepherd,
      In hymns and songs.

2. As much as you can, boldly laud him,
   For you are insufficient to praise
   Him who is greater than all praise.

23. Good Shepherd, true bread,
    Jesus have mercy on us.
    Nourish us, watch over us,
    Make us see your goodness
       In the land of the living.

EXERCISE

After singing and carefully examining the suggested motets, write a brief motet in four voices using the following text, Latin or English, or one of your own choosing. Divide the text into phrases; write an opening point of imitation and continue to a cadence which involves dovetailing of the reentry of parts with the second phrase. Use the devices of the style. The length and form should be similar to Example 9-5.
   Text: Be-ne-dic-tus es Do-mi-ne
         (Blessed are thou, O Lord
         In fir-ma-men-to cae-li.
         in the firmament of heaven.)

Example 9-9
Palestrina: *Super flumina Babilonis* (motet)

Example 9-10
Palestrina: *Lauda Sion* (motet)

10
Counterpoint in More Than Four Voices: The Mass

Aspects of Texture, Form, Text Setting

It is in the polyphonic writing for five and more parts that the contrapuntal skills of sixteenth-century composers are most abundantly revealed. The intricate interweaving of melodies in the denser textures gives opportunity for striking contrasts in passages where fewer voices are employed, while the presence of complete triads in the homorhythmic passages adds to the general richness of the sound.

In five and more parts, the plan of the composition is likely to include a generous number of rests, with the full choir sonority varied by lighter textures. In five- and six-voice works additional voices, designated *quintus* and *sextus* in the early printed editions, were generally for soprano or tenor range. In the original manuscripts without part designations the clef sign and the range would be sufficient to suggest an appropriate voice type.

Any member of the triad is doubled except a leading tone or other note raised by musica ficta, or a final third. Suspensions are not doubled, but other dissonances may be combined if their normal movement within stylistic restrictions is not disturbed. Upper and lower neighboring tones, or ascending and descending passing tones may, for example, occur in two voices simultaneously on the same pitch. Movement in parallel perfect intervals is not in the style, but in five or more voices a fifth sometimes moves by contrary motion to another fifth. Also, the octave and the unison may be approached by similar motion, one voice by step, the other by leap. The final cadence approach of Palestrina's motet, *O lux et decus Hispaniae,* illustrates the doubling and use of dissonances. The 4–3 suspension in augmentation reduces the speed for the cadence approach and allows the inner voices to reposition for movement into the final chord. The 4–3 is the suspension most often used in five and more voices.

Example 10-1
Palestrina: *O lux et decus Hispaniae* (motet)

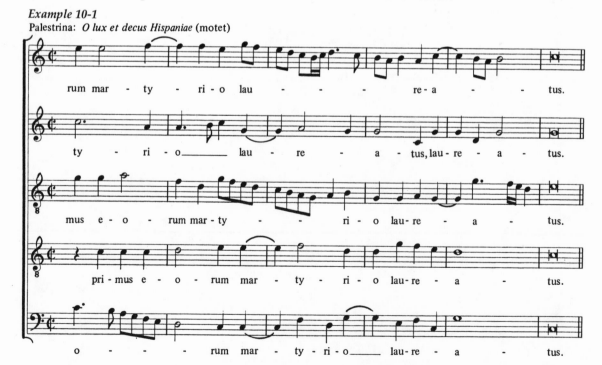

There are many compositions entirely in five and more voices. There are also those that add a voice for a section, as, for example, in the final Agnus-Dei in a Mass. The denser texture gives the ending of the Mass a sense of grandeur and finality. An imitative work in five or more voices usually begins with points of imitation widely spaced so that the first voice has completed the subject before the other voices enter. That is not always the case, however, as shown in the following points of imitation.

Example 10-2
Victoria: Sicut locutus est *(Magnificat tertii toni)*

The setting of the *Penitential Psalms* of Lasso is a rich resource in compositions for five and six voices. The verses, or motets, offer a variety of textures, moods, humour, and religious fervor. Throughout, a wealth of melodies, varied and contrasting rhythms, and expressive combinations of polyphony and chordal writing portray the nature of the text and the mastery of the composer.

Below are listed a few of the motets in five and six voices with comments on features for analysis and singing.

Psalm I, in the Dorian mode.

Verse 5 (p. 24). All five voices are active throughout, with only four instances of brief rests. Opening points of imitation are mirrored, the bass descending a tenth on the word *morte* (death). Another entry on *inferno* (in hell) has each voice descending expressively to a low point in its range.

Verse 7 (p. 31) begins in triple meter. After five measures expressing the turbulence and anger of the psalmist, the meter changes to duple. The upper voices then move collectively while the bass in a different rhythm in longer notes utters the text expressive of growing old.

Verse 10 (p. 35) is homorhythmic in the opening section. On the words *valde velociter* (very quickly), short motivic bursts in all voices in markedly different and faster rhythmic patterns enter in imitation and continue in rapid succession to the end.

Psalm II, in transposed Hypodorian mode.

Verse 3 (p. 46). The opening rhythmic design in the lower voices is repeated responsively in the soprano, starting on beat three and continuing as in conversation, uniting on *inveteraverunt ossa mea* (my bones grew old). At each new point of entry each voice has an ascending leap, the bass most dramatic with an octave on the word *clamavit* (cry out). Three times the bass leaps an ascending octave.

Verse 11 (p. 65) is a humorous setting of the text "Nollite fieri sicut equus et mulus in quibus non intellectus" (Be not like a horse or mule, without understanding). As cited in chapter 6 in relation to quarter-note usage, the awkward rhythmic confusion in this passage graphically represents the mule in his lack of understanding.

Verse 13 (p. 69) is a deeply spiritual setting of the despair of the sinner. With the words *misericordia circumdabit* (but mercy shall encompass him), beginning in measure 14, the pitch area gradually rises, and the sense of despair gives way to confident hope expressed in an exquisitely beautiful ending.

Verse 16 (p. 76), *Sicut erat in principio* (as it was in the beginning), in six voices, is in a closely woven texture. The opening points of imitation in fifth relationship are on two themes, followed by a short homorhythmic passage. Short motives on *et in saecula* initiate the final section, gaining in rhythmic momentum toward the end. The bass descends by successive leaps in thirds, measures 28–30, concluding with an authentic cadence in measures 30–31, followed by a coda and a plagal cadence.

Psalm III, in the Phrygian mode.

Many of the five-voice motets in this psalm are chordal with rhythmic variation from repeated notes alternating between the voices in a rhythmic counterpoint. The cadences are all plagal and on E or A, except for one on C. Throughout the Psalm the typical clausula vera Phrygian cadence is not used except for an interior cadence in a duo.

Verse 7 (p. 94–95) has an acceleration of rhythmic activity, somewhat frothy in nature, on *illusionibus* (illusions).

Verse 23 (p. 125) opens with E–A, imitated tonally by A–E, continuing alternately in voice entry except for one entry on B–E.

Verse 24 (p. 127), *Gloria Patri,* has all five voices entering imitatively within one and a half measures. The melodic-rhythmic movement is more active than in the other sections of the psalm with the harmonic sound focused tightly around A.

Psalm IV, in the Hypophrygian mode.

Verse 10 (p. 145) opens with "Averte faciem tuam" (Turn away thy face), presented suggestively by the movement of the bass in a descending-fifth, ascending-fourth design, E–A, D–G, C–F. The concluding words are dramatically set with three separate statements of *dele* (blot out) in staggered rhythm between rests in one part at a time.

Psalm V, in the Lydian mode.

The B♭ in the key signature simplified the work of the scribe by eliminating the frequent necessity of flattening B. It does, however, require the raising of B♭ at times. The flat in the signature here does not indicate transposed Ionian.

Verse 8 (p. 179) opens with points of imitation on G–C–G–C–F in rapid succession with a nervous rhythmic pattern between the voices on *vigilavi* (I have watched). After rests in all voices, the phrase *solitarius in tecto* (alone on the housetop) is stated by two voices, the other three entering to conclude with *in tecto*.

Verse 27 (p. 211) opens with declamatory chordal movement on *ipsi peribunt* (they shall perish). The final cadence is a leading-tone cadence on C, the fifth in the outer voices of the final chord approached by descending fifth and second.

Psalm VI, in the Hypolydian mode.

This psalm of ten sections is based on the sixth Gregorian psalm tone that is heard in each verse in various voices. The reiterated chanting note A of the psalm tone affects the choice of the harmonies and also serves as an offset to other voices with melismatic character.

Verse 1 (p. 221). Four of the five voices enter imitatively within one and a half measures. The fifth voice has the psalm tone as cantus firmus. The descending octave leap in the bass to low F on *profundis* (deep) is a dramatic interpretation of the word. The chordal movement from a cadence on C, measures 7–8, to a cadence on A with C♯ in measures 9–10 is colorful.

Verse 2 (p. 222). The cantus firmus in the alto is imitated in canon at the fifth by tenor 1. The movement of the other voices against the sustaining canonic pair enriches the solemnity of the psalm.

Verse 3 (p. 224). The alto and tenor again have the psalm tone in canon, this time imitated at the fourth and inverted in the alto.

Verse 10 (p. 233), *Sicut erat*, contains melismatic movement in four of the six voices with the soprano and tenor 1 having the psalm tone in canon at the octave.

Psalm VII, in the Mixolydian mode.

Verse 4 (p. 241) begins with a beautiful chordal passage, with many of the chords in third relationship, and affected by musica ficta. On the words *in me turbatum est cor meum* (my heart is troubled within me), two of the voices begin an offbeat rhythm soon taken by others, and the serenity of the first section turns to uneasiness. The bass approaches the final cadence by descending thirds.

Verse 7 (p. 246) contains a setting of *velociter* (quickly) in an agitated rhythmic passage. It is followed by an ending of surprising abruptness. The last note is on the fourth beat of the measure, followed by a measure of rest. It clearly bespeaks the reference in the text to the fainting away of the spirit (*defecit spiritus meus*).

Verse 8 (p. 247) opens with points of imitation at the fifth. The final theme on the words *descendentibus in lacum* (go down into the pit) moves downward over a wide range in each voice, the bass descending stepwise a twelfth.

Verse 16 (p. 263), the most florid of all the final sections, begins with all six voices in points of imitation starting on G. There are two themes, two voices on a theme in long note-values ultimately taken by the other voices, and four voices on an active melismatic theme.

Psalm VIII, in the Hypomixolydian mode.

Motet 1 (p. 266) sets the portion of the text referring to praise of the Lord by heavenly beings, verses 1 through 6 of Psalm 148. It contains broad, sweeping homorhythmic passages with a brief figure in the bass in triple rhythm.

Motet 2 (p. 275) sets verses 7 through 11, expressing praise of the Lord by earthly beings. The range is generally lower, the rhythm less varied. Rests are frequent, separating items enumerated for praise, and the final section is focused around a G minor chord in contrast to the G major referring to the preceding heavenly beings.

Motet 4 (p. 285), in six voices, is largely homorhythmic with occasional brief motivic imitations. It is in three sections, the first a solemn invitation to praise the Lord, concluding with a plagal cadence on G. The second section, in triple time, begins the list of musical instruments of praise. The list is continued in the third section, and the time-values are gradually shortened, arriving at a fast syncopated rhythm on *jubilationis*, changing suddenly to longer time-values for the final injunction to praise the Lord.

In addition to the above motets suggested for study, two complete examples are provided in the following pages, which offer a further variety in contrapuntal techniques. In the first, (Example 10-3), a hymn of Palestrina, thematic material is derived from the Gregorian hymn for the feast of St. Anthony of Padua. The Gregorian melody is begun in the first-soprano part and is imitated in canon a fourth below *(subdiatessaron)* by the second soprano. Each phrase of the plainsong melody becomes a point of imitation for all voices. The final phrase of the plainsong, in longer time-values in the canonic voices, concludes with a flowing melodic extension in the other voices while the imitating voice sustains its last note, the dominant, for four measures.

Example 10-3
Palestrina: *En gratulemur hodie* (hymn)

Example 10-4 is taken from Victoria's *Magnificat quinti toni*, which begins with "Et exultavit." Victoria wrote sixteen Magnificat settings, eight beginning with "Anima mea" and containing only the odd-numbered verses, and eight beginning with "Et exultavit" and containing only the even-numbered verses. The verse setting shown here is the last one. The psalm tone is sung in canon by the two soprano voices and imitated by the tenor, while the two altos and the bass sing a countersubject consisting of a diminution of the opening theme of the other voices. So the voices are related in thematic treatment in two groups of three, all opening with the arpeggiated major triad of the fifth psalm tone. In the final two repetitions of "saeculorum Amen," the bass line is unlike its earlier movement, containing wide leaps, such as successive fifths without change of direction.

Example 10-4
Victoria: Sicut erat *(Magnificat quinti toni)*

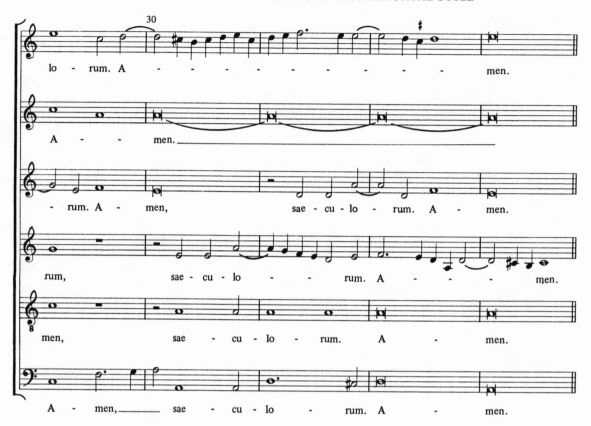

In the Masses, motets, and other compositions of Renaissance composers may be found a variety of polyphonic writing in five or more voices, much of it available in separate publications. The following works are suggested for study and singing, although their listing does not imply that others would be less rewarding.

Palestrina:

> Motets: *Alleluia tulerunt,* in 5 voices, displays an unusual return of initial theme throughout, beautiful setting of the Easter text.
>
> > *Puer qui natus est,* in 5 voices, features an interesting use of dissonance, modest vocal demands.
> >
> > *Sancta et immaculata,* in 6 voices, has canon in two voices throughout.
>
> Masses: *Repleatur os meum,* in 5 voices, contains a cycle of canons at successively smaller intervals from the octave to the unison; on a motet by Jacquet.
>
> > *Ut re mi fa sol la,* in 6 voices, in which the hexachord is the cantus firmus.

Victoria:

> Motets: *Ascendens Christus in altum,* in 5 voices, in which the opening theme ascends pictorially through an octave.

Trahe me post te, in 6 voices, has strict double canon throughout.

Masses: *Simile est regnum caelorum*, in 4 voices, in which four additional voices are introduced in the final Agnus Dei in a quadruple canon.

Ave maris stella, in 4 voices, based on plainsong, introduces an additional voice in the final Agnus Dei.

EXERCISE

Complete the counterpoint of the *Hosanna*, taken largely from Morales, given below.

Double and Triple Chorus, Polychoral Style

The Venetians—Willaert, Andrea Gabrieli, and Giovanni Gabrieli—developed the use of separated choirs, usually two or three four-voice groups. The architecture of St. Mark's Cathedral, with its two choir lofts, made the experimenting with placement of choirs appropriate. There was an organ in each of the two apses of St Mark's, and different choruses were placed there as well as elsewhere in the building. The divided choirs and the expanded possibilities of writing for them attracted composers of the period.

Although compositions may be designed for two or more groups to be performed alternately without joining forces, the polychoral style of writing more often creates a composition of two or more choirs performing separately as well as jointly, with minimal duplication of parts. In instances where the choirs join with voices of the same register singing in unison, the effect is one of increased volume, instead of the denser texture that results when voices of different spacing and lines of movement are combined.

A polychoral composition usually begins with the choirs entering separately in alternation, as though responding to each other antiphonally. As the composition continues, the choirs at times overlap, creating a dramatic thickening of texture, after which the antiphonal style resumes. The sections of combined choirs are usually brief. As they approach the end, the choirs join for a longer period, sometimes including a coda.

The main problem in writing for eight- and twelve-voice texture is the avoidance of parallel perfect intervals. Consecutive octaves and fifths are sometimes used in contrary motion in chord changes involving a common tone. Other means of circumventing parallelism include voice crossing, use of rests between chord movements, and avoidance of root movement by second. Features generally present in polychoral writing are root position chords in fifth relationships, full triads, variety of spacing between parts, and the 4–3 suspension (the suspended note is not doubled). The writing is usually in familiar style.

Two short but complete excerpts follow (examples 10-6 and 10-7), illustrating polychoral writing.

The *Hosanna* of Victoria in example 10-6 illustrates the writing for two choirs. Notice the identical repetition in the second choir of the opening phrase of the first choir. After this they are not duplicating and full eight-voice texture is present. The difficulties encountered in chord changes are handled in various ways, as for example in measure 7, when the rests in Choir II take care of consecutive octaves that would have occurred between the bass parts of the two choirs entering measure 8. In measures 8–9 and 9–10 the basses have octaves in contrary motion. In measure 9 the basses have octaves in contrary motion and again repeat the octave exchange in measures 9–10. In measure 10 the tenor parts of the two choirs are exchanged. *Hemiola* may be seen in the alto of Choir II near the end. Notice the overlapping of the ending of one choir and the entry of the other. Victoria's organ part largely duplicates Choir I.

The example of writing for three choirs, 4 + 4 + 4, is also an *Hosanna* of Victoria, this one in duple meter. The opening phrase of Choir III is followed by full twelve-voice texture. Notice the use of the common tone in the chord changes. In measure 5 the suspension on beat one in the tenor of Choir II is not doubled; rests in three voices lighten the task of distributing G and C among eleven voices. Frequent passing- and neighboring-tone dissonances in contrary motion thicken the texture. The triads of each choir are generally complete and are spaced differently from each other. The voices of Choir I are in open structure, with lower placement of tenor and bass than in the other choirs.

Example 10-6
Victoria: Hosanna *(Missa Ave Regina)*

Example 10-7
Victoria: Hosanna *(Missa Laetatus)*

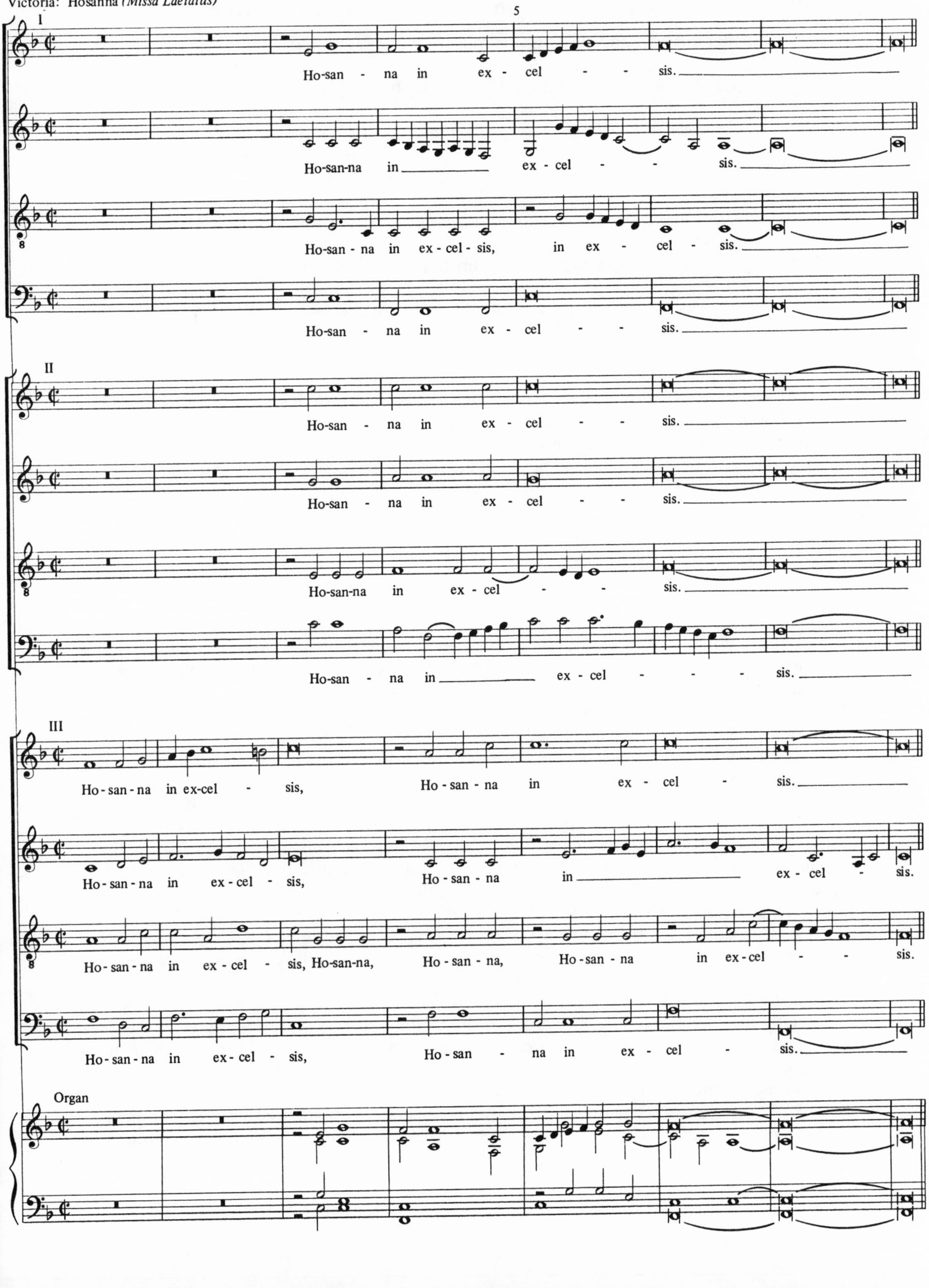

For further analysis and singing, the following are suggested:

Palestrina: *Litaniae Sacrosanctae Eucharistiae,* double chorus, two versions.

Laudate Dominum in tympanis, motet for triple chorus.

Lasso: *Omnia tempus habent,* motet for double chorus.

Laudate Dominum in tympanis, motet for triple chorus.

Victoria: *Super flumina Babylonis,* Psalm 136, for double chorus.

Ave Maria, gratia plena, motet for double chorus.

EXERCISE

After singing and carefully studying the preceding examples of eight- and twelve-voice writing, write a motet for double chorus, using the text given below. Each choir should have the first phrase alternately, the conclusion of one and the beginning of the next dovetailing. *Alleluia* should be set alternately in each choir, then repeated in eight-voice texture, the final cadence containing a 4–3 suspension. Use either the Latin or the English text.

Text: Ver-bum ca-ro fac-tum est, Alleluia, Alleluia.
(The word is made flesh, Alleluia, Alleluia.)

The Mass

The culmination of the sixteenth-century polyphonic art may be found in many of the musical settings of the Mass, the most solemn service of the Roman Catholic Church. The name (Latin, *Missa*) is derived from the final words of the liturgy, *Ite, missa est*— "Go, you are dismissed." The liturgy commemorates the Eucharist, the mystical transubstantiation of the elements into the body and blood of Christ.

The portions of the Mass whose texts vary according to the day of the liturgical year are referred to as the Proper of the Mass. Those sections that have unvarying texts are called the Ordinary of the Mass. Although the entire Mass may be said or chanted, when a composer makes a setting of the Mass, it is generally understood to be a setting of the five parts of the Ordinary: *Kyrie, Gloria, Credo, Sanctus,* and *Agnus Dei.* In the Requiem Mass (Mass for the Dead) the joyful portions, *Gloria* and *Credo,* are omitted, but composers generally include most or all of the Proper.

The polyphonic settings of the Mass are of four types:

1. The choral, or plainsong Mass, is a polyphonic setting of a Gregorian Mass Ordinary, each movement drawing its thematic material from the corresponding item of the plainsong Mass. Palestrina's *Missa pro defunctis* is an example.

2. *Cantus firmus* Mass is a Mass in which all the movements are based on one melody, usually found in the tenor. The source of the melody may be liturgical or secular and is sometimes an invented *cantus firmus.* Hymns and antiphons also provide thematic material. The Masses composed on *L'homme armé* by Josquin, Palestrina, and others are examples of the use of secular melodies.

3. Parody or Transcription Mass is based on an already existing polyphonic composition, either secular or religious. The original work, amplified, is sometimes used in its

entirety, or it may be segmented, its beginning used for the Kyrie, with other sections used later in the Mass. The text of the Mass replaces the original text. In his Mass on Sandrin's chanson, *Doulce memoire,* Lasso used largely the opening and ending sections of the original work.

4. Masses using original thematic material are few in number, for preexistent material was the favored thematic resource. A melody that was not identified with its sources may have been secular in origin, and the composer avoided acknowledging it. Therefore, any assumption that undesignated thematic material is original may be open to question.

The complete text, Latin except for Kyrie Eleison, which is Greek, with English translation and comments about polyphonic settings, follows.

Kyrie eleison, Christe eleison, Kyrie eleison.   Lord, have mercy. Christ, have mercy. Lord, have mercy.

In chant settings of this movement, each of the three prayers is sung three times, but in contrapuntal settings this is varied. The three sections are each complete, without dependence on either of the other two. The brevity of the text is compensated for in elaborate melismata, motivic imitation, and dense interweaving of cadence and entering points of imitation.

Gloria in excelsis Deo. Et in terra pax hominibus bonae voluntatis. Laudamus te. Benedicimus te, adoramus te. Glorificamus te. Gratias agimus tibi propter magnam gloriam tuam. Domine Deus, Rex caelestis, Deus Pater omnipotentens. Domine Fili unigenite Jesu Christe, Dominus Deus, Agnus Dei, Filius Patris. Qui tollis peccata mundi, miserere nobis. Qui tollis peccata mundi, suscipe deprecationem nostram. Qui sedes ad dexteram Patris, miserere nobis. Quoniam tu solus sanctus. Tu solus Dominus. Tu solus Altissimus, Jesu Christe. Cum Sancto Spiritu, in gloria Dei Patris. Amen.

Glory be to God on high, and on earth peace to men of good will. We praise thee; we bless thee; we adore thee; we glorify thee. We give thee thanks for thy great glory, O Lord God, heavenly King, God the Father almighty. O Lord, Jesus Christ, the only begotten Son: O Lord God, Lamb of God, Son of the Father, who taketh away the sins of the world, have mercy on us: who taketh away the sins of the world, receive our prayer: who sitteth at the right hand of the Father, have mercy on us. For thou only art holy: thou only art the Lord. Thou only, O Jesus Christ, are most high, together with the Holy Ghost, in the glory of God the Father. Amen.

The first phrase, "Gloria in excelsis Deo," is intoned by the priest. Because of the length of the text, passages in homorhythmic texture are frequent, allowing more words of text to be expressed in a shorter time-distance. The movement is usually in two sections with a well-defined cadence before the second section begins on "Qui tollis." The words *cum Sancto Spiritu* are often set briefly in triple time.

Credo in unum Deum, Patrem omnipotentem, factorem caeli et terrae, visibilium omnium, et invisibilium. Et in unum Dominum Jesum Christum, Filium Dei unigenitum. Et ex Patre natum ante omnia saecula. Deum de Deo, lumen de lumine, Deum verum de Deo vero. Genitum, non factum, consubstantialem Patri: per quem omnia facta sunt. Qui propter nos homines et propter nostram salutem de-

scendit de caelis. Et incarnatus est de Spiritu Sancto ex Maria Virgine: Et homo factus est. Crucifixus etiam pro nobis: sub Pontio Pilato passus, et sepultus est. Et resurrexit tertia die, secundum Scripturas. Et ascendit in caelum: sedet ad dexteram Patris. Et iterum venturus est cum gloria, judicare vivos et mortuos: cujus regni non erit finis. Et in Spiritum Sanctum, Dominum, et vivificantem: qui ex Patre Filioque procedit. Qui cum Patre et Filio simul adoratur, et conglorificatur: qui locutus est per Prophetas. Et unam sanctam catholicam et apostolicam Ecclesiam. Confiteor unum baptisma in remissionem peccatorum. Et exspecto resurrectionem mortuorum. Et vitam venturi saeculi. Amen.

I believe in one God, the Father almighty, maker of heaven and earth, and of all things visible and invisible. And in one Lord Jesus Christ, the only begotten Son of God, born of the Father before all ages; God of God, light of light, true God of true God; begotten, not made; of one substance with the Father; by whom all things were made. Who for us men, and for our salvation, came down from heaven; and was incarnate by the Holy Ghost, of the Virgin Mary; and was made man. He was crucified also for us, suffered under Pontius Pilate, and was buried. And the third day he rose again according to the scriptures; and ascended into heaven. He sitteth at the right hand of the Father; and he shall come again with glory to judge the living and the dead; and his kingdom shall have no end. And I believe in the Holy Ghost, the Lord and giver of life, who proceedeth from the Father and the Son, who together with the Father and the Son is adored and glorified; who spoke by the prophets. And I believe in one holy, catholic, and apostolic Church. I confess one baptism for the remission of sins. And I await the resurrection of the dead, and life of the world to come. Amen.

The first phrase, "Credo in unum Deum," is intoned by the priest. Passages in homorhythmic treatment, as in the Gloria, are generally included. "Et incarnatus est" is frequently given a sustained chordal texture; the words "Et resurrexit tertia die" and "Et exspecto resurrectionem mortuorum" are sometimes set in triple time. The movement is usually divided into three sections, the second beginning with *Crucifixus*, often with fewer voices, the third with *Et in Spiritum Sanctum*, often in triple time. The concluding Amen may be melismatic. The Amen of the Credo of Palestrina's *Missa Papae Marcellus* and Lasso's *Missa Doulce memoire* are beautiful examples of such settings.

Sanctus, Sanctus, Sanctus, Dominus Deus Sabaoth. Pleni sunt caeli et terra gloria tua. Hosanna in excelsis. Benedictus qui venit in nomine Domini.
Hosanna in excelsis.

Holy, Holy, Holy, Lord God of hosts. Heaven and earth are full of thy glory. Hosanna in the highest. Blessed is he that cometh in the name of the Lord.
Hosanna in the highest.

The text is divided into four sections: *Sanctus*, *Hosanna*, *Benedictus*, and repeat of *Hosanna*. The first section consists of two parts, *Sanctus* and *Pleni sunt caeli*. The setting is one of extensive polyphonic treatment. The *Benedictus* is likely to use fewer voices, frequently omitting the lowest part. The *Hosanna* is often set in a homorhythmic style, and in triple meter.

Agnus Dei, qui tollis peccata mundi: miserere nobis.

Lamb of God, who takest away the sin of the world, have mercy on us.

Agnus Dei, qui tollis peccata mundi: dona nobis pacem.

Lamb of God, who takest away the sin of the world, grant us peace.

This movement of the Mass consists of three sections, the first sung twice, concluding with *miserere nobis*, and the third concluding with *dona nobis pacem*. In musical settings the first section is usually not repeated, thereby causing the movement to be in two sections. Sometimes the second section contains an additional voice. Extensive polyphonic activity is typical throughout this concluding movement.

Suggested examples of Masses to analyze and sing:

Palestrina: *Missa Assumpta est Maria* (a 6), is a parody of his own motet.

Missa Papae Marcelli (a 6), on original material, conformed to the tenets of the Council of Trent.

Missa L'homme armé (a 5), the earlier of his two masses on this theme, is based on a secular cantus firmus.

Missa Ad fugam (a 4), in which each movement consists of two two-part canons superimposed on one another, except for the *Pleni* and *Benedictus*, which are three-part canons, and the final *Agnus Dei*, which contains a three-part canon over a two-part canon, a fifth voice having been added.

Lasso: *Missa Dixit Joseph* (a 6), is a parody of his own motet.

Missa Doulce memoire (a 4), is a parody of a chanson by Sandrin.

Missa Susanne un iour (a 5), is based on his own chanson.

Victoria: *Missa O magnum mysterium* (a 4), is a parody of his own motet.

Missa Surge propera (a 5), is a parody of a motet by Palestrina.

Missa Pro Victoria (a 9), for two choirs with an additional soprano and organ: a parody on Janequin's *La guerre*, this is the only work of Victoria built on secular material. It forecasts the style of the early Baroque.

Bibliography

Andrews, Hilda K. *An Introduction to the Technique of Palestrina.* London: Novello, 1958.

Apel, Willi. *The Notation of Polyphonic Music 900–1600,* 5th edition. Cambridge, Mass.: Medieval Academy of America, 1961.

Bank J. A. *Tactus, Tempo and Notation in Mensural Music from the 13th to the 17th Century.* Amsterdam, 1972.

Boetticher, Wolfgang. "New Lassus Studies." In *Aspects of Medieval and Renaissance Music: A Birthday Offering to Gustave Reese.* Edited by Jan La Rue. New York: W. W. Norton, 1966.

Boyd, Malcolm. *Palestrina's Style: A Practical Introduction.* London: Oxford University Press, 1973.

Brown, Howard Mayer. *Music in the Renaissance.* London: Oxford University Press, 1976.

Caldwell, John. "Musica Ficta." *Early Music* 13, no. 3 (1985): 407–8.

Cummings, Anthony M. "Toward an Interpretation of the Sixteenth-Century Motet." *Journal of the American Musicological Society* 34 (Spring 1981): 43–59.

Frei, Walter. "Die Bayerische Hofkapelle unter Orlando di Lasso." *Die Musikforschung* 15 (1962): 352–64.

Fux, Johann Joseph. *The Study of Counterpoint.* Translated and edited from *Gradus ad Parnassum* [1725] by Alfred Mann. New York: W. W. Norton, 1965.

Gauldin, Robert. *A Practical Approach to Sixteenth-Century Counterpoint.* Englewood Cliffs, N.J.: Prentice-Hall, 1985.

Gossett, P. "The Mensural System and the *Choralis Constantinus.*" *Studies in Renaissance and Baroque Music in Honor of Arthur Mendel.* Kassel: Bärenreiter, 1974.

Jeppesen, Knud. *Counterpoint: The Polyphonic Vocal Style of the Sixteenth Century.* Translated by Glen Haydon. Englewood Cliffs, N.J. Prentice-Hall, 1939.

————. *The Style of Palestrina and the Dissonance.* Translated by Margaret Hamerik. London: Oxford University Press, 1946. Reprint. New York: Dover Publications, 1970.

Kerman, Joseph. "Byrd's Settings of the Ordinary of the Mass." *Journal of the American Musicological Society* 32 (Fall 1979): 408–39.

Krenek, Ernst. *Modal Counterpoint in the Style of the Sixteenth Century.* London: Boosey and Hawkes, 1959.

Marshall, Robert. "The Paraphrase Technique of Palestrina in His Masses Based on Hymns." *Journal of the American Musicological Society* 16 (Fall 1963): 347–72.

Merrit, Arthur T. *Sixteenth Century Polyphony.* Cambridge: Harvard University Press, 1939.

Morris, R. O. *Contrapuntal Technique in the Sixteenth Century.* London: Oxford University Press, 1922.

Reese, Gustave. *Music in the Renaissance.* New York: W. W. Norton, 1954.

Roche, Jerome. *Lassus.* London: Oxford University Press, 1982.

———. *Palestrina's Style: A Practical Introduction.* London: Oxford University Press, 1973.

Routley, Nicholas. "A Practical Guide to *Musica Ficta.*" *Early Music* 13, no. 1 (1985): 59–71.

Soderlund, Gustave Frederic. *Direct Approach to Counterpoint in Sixteenth-Century Style.* Englewood Cliffs, N.J.: Prentice-Hall, 1947.

Swindale, Owen. *Polyphonic Composition.* London: Oxford University Press, 1962.

Zarlino, Gioseffo. *The Art of Counterpoint,* Part Three of *Le Istitutioni harmoniche,* 1558. Translated by Guy A. Marco and Claude V. Palisca. New Haven: Yale University Press, 1968.

———. *On the Modes,* Part Four of *Le Istitutione harmonische,* 1558. Translated by Vered Cohen and edited by Claude V. Palisca. New Haven: Yale University Press, 1983.

List of Musical Examples

Index